THE
ART
GAME

Robert Wraight

SIMON AND SCHUSTER
NEW YORK

For SMUDGE,
my silent, one-eyed critic,
who helped more than he can say

Acknowledgments

For fear of leaving someone out I shall not attempt to list here all those people who have helped me in the writing of this book. There are, however, several who, by their actions or their writing, wittingly or unwittingly contributed so much in the way of stimulation (not to say inspiration) that it would be discourteous to refrain from naming them. They are: Mr. Peter Wilson, chairman of Sotheby's; Mr. Gerald Reitlinger; Mr. Richard H. Rush; Mr. Ben Shahn; Miss Peggy Guggenheim; Mr. C. Blok; the late Lord Duveen; Mr. Terence Mullaly, art critic of the *Daily Telegraph;* the late M. Charles Baudelaire; Miss Dore Ashton.

Contents

INTRODUCTION *by Marshall B. Davidson*   9

PREFACE   13

1 ROYAL MAGPIES AND COMMON MARMOTS   19

2 ART FOR MONEY'S SAKE   30

3 TOMORROW'S WINNERS   40

4 AMERICAN WINNERS?   62

5 SNARES AND PITFALLS   71

6 FORGERIES, FAKES AND FIDDLES   79

7 RING-A-RING O' ROGUES   106

8 DISCOVERIES AND HOW TO DISCOVER THEM   117

9 THE SHOTGUN WEDDING   127

10 DEALERS, GEESE AND GOLDEN EGGS   147

11 CRITICS, ET CETERA   164

12 THE ARTNAPPERS   177

13 INSTANT ARTISTS   188

14 THE NEXT REVOLUTION   199

EPILOGUE: WILL THE BOOM LAST?   211

BIBLIOGRAPHY   217

INDEX   219

[*Picture sections follow pages 32 and 96*]

Introduction

On one of the following pages Mr. Wraight makes the point that most art critics today seem to be writing exclusively for other inmates of their own "precious little asylum"—a point it would be hard to deny. Anyone who chooses to read what else he has to say about the "art game" will quickly realize that the author, a practiced and estimable critic, stands well outside the walls of that booby hatch. He has written a book that can be read for both pleasure and profit, even by those who know nothing about art but who may know what they like—or by those who may care nothing at all about art as such, for that matter.

Even people in the latter category often get involved with art these days. In fact, almost all of us have become inescapably involved in the art world, from the time we are helpless little schoolchildren, dutifully shepherded by teachers through the halls of our proliferating museums, until the day when, grown older and more affluent, we turn an acquisitive eye to the booming art market. Since almost anything seems to qualify as art nowadays, many more people are trying their hand at turning it out than would have dreamed of the possibility in any earlier society.

Mr. Wraight is an Englishman, and he writes from a part of the world, in and about London, where practices and dealings in art boast a long and colorful history. In late years, of course, the United States—most specifically, New York—has become the epicenter of this commerce. Casting his seasoned eye across the Atlantic in turn (where Sotheby's now shares its fortunes with Parke-Bernet and many English dealers have set up shop), the author sees the same old game he has watched abroad being played with increased vigor and on an expanding scale, and he certainly is right.

In New York, at least, it is a mean neighborhood that does not have its art galleries. As another critic has observed, the yellow pages of a recent Manhattan telephone directory gave about the same amount of space to "Art Galleries and Dealers" (more than 400 listings—and this did not include auction houses and other closely related enterprises) as it did to "Bakeries, Retail." I have not checked the current directory, but from personal observation I suspect that the art galleries and dealers may by now out-number the bakeries. If art has not replaced bread as the primary staff of life, it seems to be at least equally salable merchandise. Art galleries, of course, fold up now and then, but so do bakeries; and I have seen at least one deserted bakery converted into an art gallery, but not the reverse.

There have been patrons and collectors of art since the days of the Pharaohs and the kings of Sumer; there were public collections of a sort in ancient Greece; and at least two thousand years ago Rome had its art quarter devoted to dealers as well as to forgers, fakers, and auction rooms (where the sales were sometimes rigged). But never in the past has there been anything quite like the art world of today as Mr. Wraight describes it. It may never be the same again either, for, as the author sharply observes, the nature of art itself is changing at a galloping pace. Even the individual art object these days often changes its coloration and pattern as we look at it. By the design of their creators some such contrivances even blow up or break down while we watch.

In the meantime it remains true that there is no business like the art business. In its more speculative aspects today's art market may resemble the stock market, but there is one important difference. There is nothing like the Securities and Exchange Commission to keep a watchful eye on the buying and selling, the advertising and the promoting of art. Some effort has been made lately in New York to set up effective controls, but nothing of consequence has yet come of it. The "game," as Mr. Wraight terms it, remains full of hazards and penalties, not necessarily because dealers, auction houses, and speculators are high-pressured or dishonest (although that may be a factor), but largely because so many who would like to play are ignorant or inexperienced, or may be too prone to wishful thinking.

If there are no effective controls to protect the innocent, there are nevertheless helpful guides—basic rules—for those who wish to play the game. As a student, artist, critic, collector, and dealer, Mr. Wraight has been an interested witness of and participant in these matters; he offers his counsel with candor and from experience, some of it sad. Like even the shrewdest of collectors, he has been "had" both in the auction room and in the gallery; and he has also made his *coups*. He has studied the risks that have led him and innumerable others ruefully to reckon their mistakes and count their losses or happily to enjoy their treasures. He is even bold—or rash—enough to advise you where to put your money for short-, medium-, or long-term investment, if that is the way you choose to play the game; and, as the author observes, buying pictures for love of art is virtually a thing of the past.

Mr. Wraight's story is rich in entertaining and revealing anecdote—and in modern social history for that matter. Some of the most exciting contemporary drama is being enacted in the auction houses—such as that ludicrously complicated happening at Christie's in 1965, described later, when after a few moments of utter confusion Rembrandt's portrait of Titus was finally knocked down to Mr. Norton Simon for well over two million dollars. If you understand the conventions of the auction house and the plot of a particular performance, this sort of entertainment can be as fascinating as anything on Broadway. If you are bidding, of course, the price of entertainment can be exorbitantly high.

Mr. Wraight describes and interprets such goings-on in the art world, including the current vogue for "artnapping" and ransoming, with wit and a completely understandable cynicism. Yet, as he himself confesses, his disillusionment is by no means complete. My own interest in his book stems mainly from the author's apparent solid sense of values and his sensitive appreciation of the place of art in our lives. Without these qualities he could not have written so perceptively of the skulduggery and hocus-pocus that both confuses and enlivens the contemporary scene. As a commentary on modern art—and modern attitudes toward art—this book has a lot more to recommend it than many of the formal art histories and volumes on art appreciation that are run off the presses in such profusion these days.

MARSHALL B. DAVIDSON

Preface

Artwise, as an American millionaire collector said to me, we live in a remarkable age. An age in which £800,000 is a bargain price for a "battered, browned, overworked and fuzzed cartoon" (the words are Mr. Gerald Reitlinger's, not mine) and a washbasin is exhibited as a work of art (or anti-art?) at the Tate Gallery. An age in which a stapling-machine manufacturer's wife pays £63,000 for a commode to make her husband's life more exciting when he gets home from the factory and a leading artist of the "Happenings Movement" fills a Paris gallery from floor to ceiling with cartloads of the city's refuse.

Never before has there been so great an interest in art. Never before has the interest on art investments been so great. Never before has art been considered so important a part of education. Never before has education been considered so unimportant a part of art. Never have there been so many artists and art students. Never have there been so many bad artists and art students. Never have so many good and bad books on art poured from the presses or so many reproductions of good and bad pictures been stuck on walls. Never has art been such big business and never has big business attracted so many speculators who want to get in on the act. In fact the art game has become a vast confidence trick for which there is an ever-lengthening queue of willing victims begging to be fleeced. It is said not only that man cannot live by bread alone, but that he cannot live without art. But it is pure cant to pretend that he needs the precious-object-in-the-gilt-frame sort of art that is the prize in the art game. A painting has no intrinsic value. It is a luxury commodity for which a market is deliberately created and maintained by financially interested parties who are neither more nor less noble than the operators of any other legal sort of market. The market value of art is as artificial as that of gold or of diamonds. The great public galleries are the Fort Knoxes of art. Their contents, unseen by the vast majority of the world's population, control the price of art outside them just as surely as the value of money is governed by those obscene, illogical and ludicrous hoards of gold. In a utopian world all the Fort Knoxes, of gold or of art, would be abolished. The gold would be used only for filling teeth or making ornaments. The pictures would be given away, one to every person or family. One really good painting in a man's home will do more for him (and maybe for art) than thousands hidden away in the great public mausoleums and in the basements of dealers' galleries.

In my heart I applaud the sentiments of British artist Jack Smith, who, when it was suggested that he had come from Sheffield to London because it is easier to sell paintings in the capital, replied: "That's true. But, oh! This business of selling paintings, and all the ridiculous false values that are placed on works of art. I would like all paintings to be free. I would like the artist to be given an annual salary so that his paintings could be given away to anybody who wanted them. Why not? A good painting is priceless and nobody can afford it really. But also, in the monetary sense of the word, it is valueless. Therefore I would like to take the money element out of art so that perhaps painting would be viewed in rather different terms."*

In spite of this I am, as is Mr. Smith, a player (one of the "etceteras"—see Chapter Eleven, "Critics, et Cetera") in the art game, and it is therefore to my material benefit to see that the game goes on being played, at least for the rest of my lifetime. Hence the reason for this book, which is intended to attract recruits to the game and to help those recruits to decide which rat hole (I meant to write "art" there, but my typewriter, which refuses to mince words, wrote "rat") to choose. It is not another book about the aesthetics or the history of art. It is largely a book about the many and various ways in which money is made out of art and, it follows, the many and various ways of losing money in art. It is not for the high-minded, but for those who think that art, like sex, should not be taken too seriously. A contemptible book? Perhaps. But before you put it back on the shelf just answer this questionnaire:

1. When you see the latest thing in avant-garde art, do you say:

(a) "It can't be just a leg-pull"?
Or (b) "It's just a leg-pull"?
Or (c) "I could pull legs like that"?

* Noël Barber, *Conversations with Painters.*

2. When you read about a forger who has fooled the art experts, do you say:

    (a) "How terrible"?
Or (b) "How funny"?
Or (c) "How clever"?

3. If a "knocker" (see Chapter Six, "Forgeries, Fakes and Fiddles") came to your home and offered a hundred pounds for that worthless little picture Grandmother left you, would you:

    (a) Tell him it is not for sale at any price?
Or (b) take his money?
Or (c) put him off until you can get an expert valuation of it?

4. When the Royal Academy offered the British nation Leonardo da Vinci's cartoon *The Virgin, Saint Anne and the Infant Christ with Saint John* for £800,000, would you, if you were a Briton,

    (a) Have sent a donation *anonymously* to the Appeal Fund?
Or (b) said, "What a waste of the taxpayers' money"?
Or (c) thought, "If it were mine I would have sold it in America for twice as much"?

If your answers to all four questions are *a*, then by all means put the book down at once and keep your illusions. If all of your answers are *b*, it is not for you, either. You are not such stuff as the art game is played on. But if all, or any, of your answers are *c*, the book is yours. Work hard at it and you can join the game. However low (or high) you may be there is a place for you, if you really try, among the collectors, the investors, the dealers, the runners, the knockers, the auctioneers, the experts, the critics, the art historians, the museum wallahs, the art-gossipmongers, the forgers, the publicists, the phony art teachers, the culture hawkers, the vendors of artists' materials and of painting holidays, the pseudo Impressionists, the "pupils of Annigoni," the rubbish collagists, the neoprimitives and, last and least likely, the PBGA.*

Don't lose any time, because, as artist-critic Ad Reinhardt, the "black monk" of the New York school, prophesies, *"The next revolution in Art will see the disappearance of personal art-dealing, private art-collecting and individual artist-enterprising, of personalistic, privateering art—'pricing, buying and selling.'"*†

Now read on.

---

* The poor bloody genuine artists.

† Ad Reinhardt, "The Next Revolution in Art," in *Art News* (New York), Feb. 1964.

Art is well known as a game in which one pays for the right to hang on his walls someone else's mental troubles embodied in paint. A game which more often than not leads to expense and fascinates its small circle of devotees who are all convinced that the world needs it, whilst those outside the circle are equally convinced that it does not. As a game art makes sense as long as the entire circle joins in. It stops doing so, at the same time revealing its true nature, as soon as somebody violates the rules, e.g. when Marcel Duchamp submitted a urinal bearing the signature R. Mutt for an exhibition. If the artist is to have his soul's dirty linen publicly cherished then why not his urinal? Or, for that matter, the contents of his urinal, as Piero Manzoni pointed out.

–C. BLOK,
GEMEENTE MUSEUM, THE HAGUE,
IN *ICA Bulletin*, NO. 138/9

1

Royal
Magpies
and
Common
Marmots

To collect nothing at all is to descend below the level of magpies and marmots.
—Gerald Reitlinger,
The Economics of Taste

Without covetousness you are not going to have an appreciation of art. And I think that if covetousness by some magic was destroyed art would come to an end. It's very rare to be able to appreciate art without wanting to own it.
—Peter Wilson,
chairman of sotheby's,
in an interview on the
BBC Third Programme

A collector is someone interested in art for his own self-ennoblement. Nowadays people buy paintings mostly out of snobbery or to avoid tax.
—Peggy Guggenheim,
Confessions of an Art Addict

The art game is very old. The Greeks played it and the Romans played it. In more modern civilizations it was first played only by kings and great noblemen. Henry VIII played a rudimentary form of it, but Charles I, who acquired a taste for collecting from his older brother, Henry, Prince of Wales, was the first royal "division one" player in England. He is said to have had a "good nose" for pictures (there were two Rembrandts in his collection while the artist was still young and little known), and he employed a team of agents to scour Europe, and particularly Italy, for new acquisitions. Usually the activities of these agents were shrouded in a

cloak-and-dagger air of mystery for fear of such rival collectors as
Cardinal Richelieu and the Grand Duke of Tuscany. He encouraged his courtiers to make him gifts of paintings and his ambas-
sadors to bring paintings back to him from their trips abroad.
Sometimes he would make exchanges with other collectors, a
Leonardo for a Holbein and a Titian, a volume of Holbein portraits for Raphael's *Saint George.* By his virtuoso gamesmanship
he amassed, in the space of twenty years, an almost incomparable
collection.

Then along came Cromwell, and after the King's execution in
1649 the collection was confiscated by the Commonwealth. An
inventory was made in which each picture was valued, and then
the dispersal of the collection began. First a number of works
were reserved by Cromwell for official purposes. Among them
were the great Raphael cartoons now in the Victoria and Albert
Museum, which were valued at £300. A second group of pictures
was allotted to be used to pay various creditors of the Court, and
a third group was offered for sale. Many of the pictures in the
second group were never collected but remained in the palaces
until the Restoration, when, with these unclaimed works as a
nucleus, Charles II began his efforts to rebuild his father's collection.

The job was an impossible one. Most of the greatest treasures
in the third group had been bought by dealers and sold to such
European collectors as the King of Spain, the Archduke Leopold
William of Austria and Cardinal Mazarin. Among them were
Giorgione's *Concert Champêtre* and a superb collection of Titians,
all now in the Louvre, Raphael's *La Perla,* now in the Prado, and
many of today's most prized masterpieces in the great museums
of other European countries. But if these things were out of
Charles's reach, others, bought by English collectors, were not.
A royal commission, whose methods were, to put it mildly, un-
ethical, was set up to direct the recovery.

Acting upon reports supplied by special informers the commission brought certain pressures to bear which provoked such a flow of "gifts" to the King that numerically, at least, a major part of the royal collection was reconstituted.

To paraphrase art historian Wilhelm von Bode's comment on the American banker Pierpont Morgan, Charles II was the first Englishman who was determined to possess everything of the best, if it was not already in private hands. Indeed, even if it was already in private hands; for although the rules of the art game have become more complicated and the number of players has vastly increased, the principal goal was then, as now, to provide people who already had all the necessities of life with an overt way of showing who were the top dogs. Keeping up with the Joneses artwise was, in the seventeenth century, a matter of keeping up with the Stuarts. Then, as now, it thrived on covetousness and snobbery. Only the quality of the snobbery has changed. The change, from a predominantly intellectual snobbery to a predominantly "money" snobbery, came about, according to Ernst Fischer, with the growth of capitalism:

For the capitalist, luxury may mean the purely private satisfaction of his desires, but it also means the chance of displaying his wealth for prestige reasons. Capitalism is not essentially a social force that is well-disposed to art or that promotes art; in so far as the average capitalist needs art at all, he needs it as an embellishment of his private life or else as a good investment.*

Such a capitalist collector was Russian-born John Julius Angerstein, "the father of the modern Lloyd's," whose pictures, bought by Parliament after his death in 1823, formed the foundation of

---

* Ernst Fischer, *The Necessity of Art: A Marxist Approach.*

the National Gallery. Of him Sir Philip Hendy, the present director of the National Gallery, has written:

It has been said that he was a new type of collector in that his acquisition of pictures was also an acquisition of prestige. His was certainly
not the first collection which was intended to bring prestige to its
owner; but as a self-made man of foreign birth "considered deficient
in Education" he may well have relied on his pictures to express something that he did not know how to express himself. They were certainly
the chief instrument of the peculiar position which he made for himself "at the West End of the town." Several of the leading artists and
collectors were often to be found at 100 Pall Mall, where he kept open
house and hospitable board and built a gallery for his collection. As
the collection increased, more and more visitors were allowed to see
it, until not to have seen Mr. Angerstein's pictures was to be socially
unfinished.*

One hundred years after Angerstein, the astonishing Joseph
Duveen was to exploit, on a vast scale, the capitalists' demand for
prestige-giving art which by then had flowered mightily in America. Duveen's enormous success as a dealer lay in the fact that he
understood better than any dealer before him the nature of the
hunger for prestige experienced by the great capitalist emperors.
He knew because he had the hunger himself. He was no great art
expert, he had no need to be, he could afford to hire any expert he
liked, but as a practical psychologist he was, and still is, without
an equal in the art game. He knew, in the first place, that if you
are selling prestige it is no good offering it cheap. In a society in
which prestige is based on money, the more you pay the more you
get. It followed, too, that the more *he* paid the more prestige *he*
got. For this reason he delighted in publicity. Not for him the
secret deal. Whether he was buying or selling he let the facts be

---

* Philip Hendy, *The National Gallery, London.*

known as widely as possible. "When you pay high for the price-less, you're getting it cheap," he told his millionaire clients and then conditioned them to the privilege, as one of them put it, of paying a premium for the privilege of paying the highest prices for the priceless.

In his superb book *Duveen*, S. N. Behrman tells anecdote after anecdote illustrating the almost childlike faith that these great tycoons had in Duveen. There was H. E. Huntington confessing to a member of Duveen's staff that if Duveen told him a pair of ordinary andirons were remarkable and worth $75,000 he would gladly pay up. There was Jules Bache gratefully agreeing to guarantee Duveen a 100 per cent profit on anything the dealer deigned to offer him. There was Henry Clay Frick overcome by Duveen's generosity in letting him have a Gainsborough for $300,000 and overlooking the fact that if Duveen had not deliberately outbid Knoedler's, who, he knew, were acting for Frick, he would have got it much cheaper. And there was the great Andrew Mellon thanking Duveen for letting him buy the contents of his apartment—for twenty-one million dollars. To all of these, and dozens of other millionaire collectors whose thirst for prestige art he set out to slake at prices even higher than those of today, Duveen presented himself as a Saint Peter through whose grace alone they could get passes, albeit very expensive ones, to immortality. He seemed able to turn every general adversity to his personal advantage. When taxation and death duties threatened to end the millionaires' picture-buying bonanza he showed his clients that:

the public bequest, impervious to taxation, was the way out. Specifically, the public bequest of Duveen's was the way out. By earmarking his purchases for museums, a collector could afford to buy art; at least he could let art pass through his hands on the way to the museums from Duveen. Gifts to museums offered his clients not merely economy but immortality. Using Duveen's method an aged American millionaire could, in good conscience, circumvent oblivion and the Collector of Internal Revenue at a single stroke. Under Duveen's spell, one after another of his clients—H. E. Huntington, Frick, Mellon, Bache, Kress —took up this form of philanthropy. For Duveen the advantage was double; with museums as the terminal for his pictures, he no longer had to worry about the passing of the big houses—the museums were larger than the houses—and he no longer had to worry that the pictures would be dumped back on the market at a time when it might be difficult for him to sell them, especially at the prices he would have to charge after buying them back at Duveen prices.

The American "public bequest" system, whereby a private citizen who buys works of art gets a substantial tax concession if he undertakes to leave those works of art to a museum when he dies, has had a very far-reaching effect on the art game. In the first place it meant that American collectors had a financial advantage over other collectors. They were given what amounted to a government subsidy, which, like any subsidy given to purchasers rather than sellers, led to an increase in prices. But it did much more than that. It made the art market attractive to a new type of collector, one who cared nothing about art and was interested initially not even in its prestige-giving properties, but in its tax-exemption possibilities. Having joined in the art game, such a "collector" would then, of course, discover that it offered much more than tax exemption and begin to learn to enjoy those others of art's present built-in boons—prestige and profit. By comparison with the new-style American collector who has come to art in this way, such men as Mellon and Morgan and Huntington were art-for-art's-sake aesthetes. This sort of collector, more than any before him, has equated the possession of works of art with the possession of money, and his example has inevitably been followed in countries where no tax-dodging inducement is offered. He is a gift to those dealers who, now that the best Old Masters and Impressionist pictures are nearly all locked up in museums, are promoting modern art and artists by every means known to modern high-pressure salesmanship.

There are still, of course, some collectors of integrity and great knowledge, even in America, but these people are not a part of the art game as it is played today. They cannot be led by the nose or made the fools of dealer-inspired fashion, but follow their own taste and conviction and get a satisfaction and pleasure that has nothing to do with the envy of others. Indeed, they are often collecting the work of artists who are unpopular and probably unknown to the type of collector who predominates today, the new-rich tycoon who has devoted his whole life to making money only to discover that he has nothing except the things that money can buy. One of these things, however, is the outward appearance of culture. And this means paintings. Almost invariably, when I have talked to any collector of this sort in Britain he has claimed at some point that he was "always interested in art as a boy." But this does not mean that he now buys the paintings he likes. (In this respect his Victorian forerunner, who paid £10,000 for a bad Landseer and 7,000 guineas for an Albert Moore in preference to an Italian primitive, was more praiseworthy.) He has probably had no time to develop even bad taste of his own and must now rely entirely on the knowledge of an expert who can tell him that such and such pictures are the ones he ought to have and can give him the assurances he wants that they are good investments. What can happen to this tycoon-type collector when he tries to go it alone is amusingly illustrated by a story I heard a few years ago of a wealthy industrialist who, after negotiating for months to buy a collection of pictures by a nineteenth-century artist called Pesaro for £20,000, suddenly lost interest. He gave no reason, but rumor had it that until the last minute he thought he was going to get several dozen Pissarros for his £20,000.

In America the collector who invests in pictures and the prestige that goes with them is generally franker than his British counterpart. "My passion is for the Impressionists, and dollarwise they are also great," said one Texas collector quoted by John Bainbridge in *The Super-Americans*. Another, when told by a friend that his collection of Picassos made him a Communist in the eyes of "local patriots," replied, "You can tell those sons of bitches over there that I've made a quarter of a million dollars on these paintings so far. That will shut them up, because that's the kind of language they understand." It is, of course the language most of us understand. It is the language of the art game. It has succeeded, where Esperanto has failed, in becoming a universal language. Whereas in the past it was spoken only in whispers by consenting art dealers in private, today it is shouted by property magnates and oilmen, grocery tycoons and shipowners, stockbrokers and washing-machine manufacturers from Bond Street to Madison Avenue, from Venice to Dallas, from Paris to São Paulo. The whole business of collecting is being so vulgarized that ultimately it must defeat its own end, and instead of being a symbol of culture a collection of what the auctioneers call "Impressionist and Modern" works of art will signify philistinism and the crudest sort of materialism.

In recent years we have seen the greatest of international art shows, the Venice Biennale, turned into a Babel-onian market at which dealers, gallery proprietors, critics, collectors and artists behave just like any other businessmen at an international trade show. The booze flows continuously for days, the expense accounts and the old pals' acts are worked overtime, deals are fixed, bribes are paid, reputations are invented, publicity stunts are thought up. But it would be wrong to think that in all this the "collector" is the poor gullible victim of rapacious dealers. He is, rather, their collaborator. He likes to pay high prices. He likes to pay high prices not for the thrill of being extravagant or for the publicity it may bring him (although both these are important to him) but because by supporting the dealer's efforts to upgrade the prices of a particular artist he is improving his own investment in that artist. There is a whole class of collectors today, as any dealer will tell you, who are not interested in getting anything cheap. They are suspicious of it. The reason is simple: The only thing they understand is money, and their admiration for any picture is almost invariably in direct proportion to the amount paid for it. They have no built-in criteria by which to judge a work of art either technically or aesthetically and are obliged to work on the assumption that the most expensive things in the world are the best. This is something we are all obliged to do to some extent when buying things of which we have no special knowledge. We are dependent almost entirely upon the honesty of the retailer who tells us that this watch is worth twice as much as that one or that this wool is far better quality than that and therefore worth paying more for. And because generally the retailer is honest these things are so. If then money is no problem we buy the most expensive of everything because we want the best. We shop in the smartest stores instead of the more modest ones, even though we may believe that the difference in quality does not wholly justify the difference in price.

The commonest type of big art collector today is a man who has vastly more money than sensibility. If he is a fool he goes around, like certain Texan collectors (they would be more correctly called "accumulators"), buying in bulk according to his own whims. (As the undiscriminating patron of living artists he may, by chance, be doing a service to contemporary art, but it is much more likely that by his lack of discrimination he is encouraging the phony and the worthless.) If he is shrewd he puts himself in the hands of a well-established dealer and lets him build up a collection for him, a collection that is primarily a sound investment and only incidentally a group of works of art.

His attitude to art has infected everyone else in the art game:

the artists, the dealers, the auctioneers, the public and private patrons, the smaller collectors, even the critics. Largely because of him the art trade has lost the last little bit of that dignity that once raised it above other forms of trade. Now it has become a business like any other for marketing a commodity at the biggest possible rate of profit.

Buying pictures for love of art is virtually a thing of the past. Constantly regaled by the press with stories about fortunes, large and small, made out of art every day, even the most ingenuous picture buyer finds himself wondering how much his picture will be worth in the future. From there it is only a short step to buying pictures with thoughts of profit uppermost in his mind. And having reached that stage there can be no going back. He cannot regain his innocence, he can only go forward inspired by the knowledge that there is easy money to be made from art by anyone who takes the trouble to learn the ropes.

The knowledge that the present boom cannot last forever will give him a sense of urgency. He will soon discover that in order to succeed there must be no more love-of-art stuff in his thinking. "Art, like business, is business," must be his motto. He will learn to stand outside art and look at it dispassionately, with cold, mean, stockbrokerish eyes, and be as objective as a butcher sizing up livestock. He will learn to recognize a new fashion in the early stages of gestation and smell the first whiff of death about a moribund one. He will learn what to buy and when and where to buy it, how much it is worth, how much to pay for it and where and for how much to sell it at any particular time. He will learn not to buy anything simply because he likes it and to buy things he hates if they look like good investments. He will learn the tricks of the trade and how to counter them with knowledge and cunning of his own or of others whose brains he can pick.

What follows is an attempt to reveal to him some of the rules of a game that has no rules. If, from time to time, I betray a lack of resolution or a lack of sympathy with some of the players it is because I was brought up to regard art as something akin to religion. Disillusionment came only in recent years and is still by no means complete.

2

Art
for
Money's
Sake

The total number of authentic, accepted paintings by Michelangelo can be counted on the fingers and we can dispense with him as part of the art market. His fresco painting in the Sistine Chapel might well be considered the most valuable work of art in the world, but we can be fairly certain that it will never be sold.
— RICHARD H. RUSH

Art as an Investment

The extraordinary quotation above (it is almost as good as Duveen's "If I had the Sistine Chapel, I could sell it tomorrow half-a-dozen times over") is taken from a book, *Art as an Investment*, published in America in 1961. The author, Richard H. Rush, is the holder of the degrees of Master of Business Administration and Doctor of Commercial Science awarded by the Harvard Graduate School of Business Administration, and is also an investment banker, an ardent amateur of art and the owner of a collection of pictures valued (in 1961) at "more than one-half million dollars." The book, widely reviewed on publication, drew from the *Wall*

30

Street Journal the comment that Mr. Rush had "almost succeeded
in applying Dow-Jones averaging techniques to the suddenly expanding world of art brokerage" but had not "quite managed to
come up with a suggestion for an 'art exchange' page that would
be equivalent to an ordinary stock exchange page, because the
6,000 extant Renoir paintings, for example, can't be averaged for
a useful ticker tape quotation"! Nevertheless, his advice was no
less valuable than that of those selfless altruists the financial
columnists, the racing tipsters and, in Britain, the football-pools
experts who, while telling us how to get rich quick, never seem
to take their own advice.

Thoughtfully, Mr. Rush did not pitch his advice in highflown
terms. Example: "His paintings of peasant life bring in the low
four figures, and his Cubist period works sometimes sell in the
low five figures." He was, pardonably, a bit shaky on British paintings and painters. After all, Gainsborough himself thought that
he ought to have been *Sir* Thomas, and if William Holman Hunt
(1827–1910) is not (along with Victor Passmore [*sic*], Stanley
Spencer, Philip Wilson Steer and Alan Reynolds!) exactly "a leading name of the Contemporary British School," well, he was once.
Less easily forgiven was his summing up of an account of Hitler's
persecution of such great artists as Kokoschka, Nolde, Kandinsky
and Klee. "The ironical part about this policy of Hitler," he wrote,
"was that while Hitler himself painted pictures and several have
appeared on the auction market recently, he painted no better
than the Expressionists"! And one's faith in his judgment was a
little shaken when, after saying that what makes an artist great
is his power to add something new to the art of painting, he cited
Annigoni, alongside Raphael, as an example of quality, "the es-
sence of art value."

Such imperfections apart, however, the book was remarkable
in several ways. It was full of hardheaded horse sense couched in
the most forthright terms completely free of that namby-pamby

aesthetics stuff. When, for instance, Mr. Rush wanted to say, "Don't put all your art eggs in one basket," he wrote:

To own just one painting is like investing all of one's assets in one stock. Standard Oil Company of New Jersey is certainly a fine company and its stock is good, but there is merit to the attitude that it might not rise as surely as would a portfolio of selected stocks. There is the additional disadvantage in owning just one painting as against owning one kind of stock: one always knows the value of the one stock, but he doesn't know the value of the one painting until he offers it for sale.

But it was remarkable chiefly because (so far as I am aware) it was the first book to come out openly and treat the art business as one might treat any other business. By means of price lists and a number of graphs it sought to give an accurate picture of all the major price movements, over the previous thirty or thirty-five years. Of these the *Wall Street Journal* remarked:

To judge by Mr. Rush's graphs, those art investors who have gone in for French post impressionism and French "modern" have done considerably better for themselves than investors in most electronics or chemical stocks. Lumping the three post impressionist leaders, Van Gogh, Gauguin and Cézanne, together for instance, Mr. Rush produces an absolutely dizzy ascending curve. Taking 1930 for his base year of 100, Mr. Rush finds the Van Gogh–Gauguin–Cézanne trio hitting 177% in 1950, 566% in 1955, and 4,833% in 1960.

Surprisingly no one who reviewed the book thought to suggest to Mr. Rush that he should now write a second volume which will tell us, not what has happened to prices in the past twenty-five years, but what is going to happen to them in the next twenty-five so that we may all invest now with confidence. In the absence of such a book I propose to give my own forecasts based mainly upon observations in the London sale rooms during recent years

Artists often make the best critics, even of their own work. Here, to prove the point, is Roger Hilton aiming a symbolic kick at his painting *March 1963*, which had just won for him the first prize of £1,500 in the John Moores Liverpool Exhibition of 1963.

Other prizewinners were Anthony Donaldson, Philip Sutton, Harold Cohen, R. Kitaj, Michael Kidner, Terry Lee, Bridget Riley, Stephen McKenna and Christopher Paice. Commenting on the exhibition as a whole Hilton said, "They are terrible pictures. No wonder mine won. I wonder what the world is coming to."

Right is a more recent work, *Painting '64*, by Roger Hilton. It is 6 ft. x 6 ft.

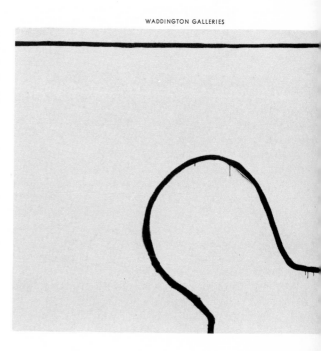

In 1964 this small, somewhat battered painting on panel of "a soldier playing a fife, another a drum and a third raising a banner" was taken to Christie's by a dealer who had bought it at a country sale for "less than fifty pounds." It proved to be a work of Pieter Breughel the Elder that had been in Charles I's collection (it bears the cipher CP [Carolus Princeps] surmounted by a crown on the reverse). Given to Charles I by his Master of the King's Bedchamber, Endymion Porter, it was sold by the Commonwealth for £5 and recovered by Charles II. The last record of it in the royal inventories is dated 1713. At Christie's it was bought by a London dealer for 23,000 guineas. A pity it was not bought by the Queen and returned to the Royal Collection. That would have done much to silence the comments, so often heard in the art world, about the Royal Family's lack of taste for, and lack of interest in, great art.

In November 1963 at Christie's the first of these two paintings by Charles Brooking (1723-1759) realized a record price of £5,460. It was the first intimation to the public that a "Brooking boom" had begun. But within four months the boom had boomed to such an extent that the virtually identical picture (Brooking often made several replicas of his pictures) shown below fetched £14,500 at Sotheby's. Some small part of this difference may have been due to a difference in quality and condition, but the second picture's price was no flash in the pan. In the same sale other seascapes by Brooking made £15,500 and £10,-500. In every case, including that at Christie's, the buyer was the London dealers Leggatt Brothers.

Which twin is the £145,000 twin? The answer is the one on the left. She cost the city of Strasbourg that much at Sotheby's in July 1963. Why did Strasbourg think she was worth so much? Because she is a superb example of the work of Nicolas de Largillière (1656–1746), because she is called *La Belle Strasbourgeoise* and wears the costume commonly worn by the young married women of Strasbourg belonging to the well-to-do bourgeoisie between 1650 and about 1730. And, presumably, because she was thought to be unique. But that was before her twin, the picture on the right, turned up immediately after the sale, in the showrooms of Frank Partridge & Sons, just across the road from Sotheby's. Both pictures are approximately 50 in. x 40 in., they are identical in every detail except the background, and both are indisputably the work of Largillière. The only major difference between them was one of price. The second version (it may have been painted first) was offered at £70,000.

French artist Jean-Pierre Schecroun demonstrating the ease with which he could produce, in three minutes, a convincing imitation of a typical Picasso bullfight drawing with brush and ink. Before he was arrested and charged with forgery in 1962, Schecroun had produced, and his accomplices had sold, about eighty works purported to be by Picasso and other modern masters. The pictures, priced at £200 to £1,200, were said to have brought in £25,000 in two years. Like so many before him Schecroun claimed that all he had wanted to do in the first place was expose the idiocy of the dealers who refused to buy his own paintings but gave ridiculous sums for work supposedly by other artists that he could do in a few minutes.

Making a bonfire of twelve fake Utrillos in a Montmartre garden is the artist's widow, Mme. Lucie Valore Utrillo. All the paintings had been sold for high prices in the Paris art market before she and art dealer Paul Pétridès, leading expert on Utrillo's work, brought an action in the French courts challenging their authenticity. As she fed the canvases to the flames Mme. Utrillo suddenly had misgivings. "I'm not sure they're fakes," she said nervously. But the experts reassured her and she went on stoking.

In Auction is a publick Sale
That impairs those who fairly deal
Whilst South Sea India Companies
Are nought but meer Monopolies

That like a certain Corporation
First bite the Poor, then gull ye Nation
Thus Fraud and Insincerity
Reign more or less in each Degree

BRITISH MUSEUM

Egbert van Heemskerck II, who painted the picture from which this engraving was made, died in England in 1744, the year in which Sotheby's was founded and twenty-two years before James Christie started the business that still bears his name. Tales of art auctions in van Heemskerck's day leave no doubt that his satire was justified. And in one respect, at least, things have not changed—the artist (that's him in the bottom left corner having his throat cut and his pocket picked simultaneously by the dealers) still gets a raw deal. Pictures that he painted and sold for a pittance may fetch a fortune in the sale room but he gets nothing from the sale. If he is still working and selling his work this is no great hardship, but if fame has come to him late in life he may have to stand by and see collectors and dealers making huge profits from the work he did in his prime. Even worse, after his death his widow and family may be suffering impoverishment while his pictures are changing hands at fancy prices. In France, a *douane morale,* under which the families of artists dead less than fifty years are paid two per cent of the selling price, does something to alleviate such hardship. The idea should be copied by other countries.

This magnificent bronze statuette of a rearing horse (23 cms. high) was bought at Christie's by Mr. Pierre Jeannerat in 1933. It was in a job lot of bronzes that cost him 11½ guineas. From the start Mr. Jeannerat was convinced that it was related to some of the many drawings of rearing horses by Leonardo da Vinci, which are in the Royal Collection at Windsor Castle and one of which is shown in the second illustration. Over the years since it was discovered by Jeannerat, his attribution of the work to Leonardo has been strengthened by the opinions of many experts, so that today its market value is anyone's guess—£100,000? £200,000? Or more?

and a consideration of a number of the many and varied factors that affect, govern and determine price changes.

The first thing that should be remembered when we read of some spectacular new record price is that we are living in an inflationary period. The devaluation of the pound since the prewar period means that today's prices must be divided by approximately four to make a real comparison with prewar prices. (For rough comparisons of American prices today's figures in dollars should be divided by three.) Comparisons with earlier periods become increasingly more difficult to make the further we go back, but some of the prices paid in the first thirty years of this century, and in the eighteenth and nineteenth centuries, show that the sort of prices that today make the public gasp are not by any means unprecedented. (What is unprecedented is the *quantity* of pictures changing hands at high prices.) Indeed, in the 1920s the great American millionaires frequently paid prices equivalent to, and often even greater than, those of today. The $750,000 that Duveen charged Alfred W. Erickson for Rembrandt's *Aristotle* in 1928 was worth much the same as the $2,300,000 for which the same picture sold at auction in New York in 1961. The $600,000 that Henry Huntington paid Duveen in 1921 for Gainsborough's *Blue Boy* was worth something like five times as much as the £130,000 Agnew's gave in 1960 for the same artist's *Mr. and Mrs. Andrews in a Park* (now in the National Gallery, London). The $1,166,000 paid by Andrew Mellon in 1931, the middle of the Great Depression, for Raphael's *Alba Madonna* was equivalent to more than a million of today's pounds.

Were such a picture as the *Alba Madonna* to be offered for sale today it would almost certainly fetch nearer two million than one million pounds, for not only is there much more money about now than there was in 1931 but there are even fewer Raphaels about. The effect of scarcity upon prices is incalculable.

It can also be ridiculous, as was seen in Britain in 1962 when the impoverished Royal Academy of Arts decided to sell by auction the Leonardo da Vinci cartoon, *The Virgin, Saint Anne and the Infant Christ with Saint John.* There was an immediate protest from those who feared that this work, known only to a small minority of the British public, would go to America. To appease the protesters the Academy offered to sell it to the British people at the "bargain price" of £800,000. But the Government was not prepared to pay and a public subscription was organized by the National Art Collections Fund. When rather more than half the required sum had been scraped together in this way, the Government provided the balance and the cartoon went into the permanent collection of the National Gallery, London. Subsequently it was made known that, had the picture gone to auction, several American museums would have been prepared to bid up to £1,500,000 for it, and at least one would have gone up to £2,000,000!

In a sense every painting has a scarcity value, because it is unique, but this scarcity value cannot be translated into terms of money until more than one person wants it (or covets it, as Peter Wilson has put it) and is prepared to pay for it. To these people the picture is to some degree a rarity in the sense that it is the one they want at a particular time, in preference to all others. A struggle between two such potential buyers who happen to have large financial resources is usually behind the freak price that hits the headlines. Thus two individuals (where dealers are bidding for extremely expensive pictures they are usually acting for a client or have a particular client in mind) whose reasons for wanting a particular painting may be the most personal and may have very little to do with art, may yet become price fixers of a particular artist's work and the creators of a fashion.

Two examples of this come immediately to mind. The first was in 1957, when the Greek shipowner Stavros Niarchos, bidding, so it is said, against another Greek shipowner who is related to him,

paid 100,000,000 francs (£104,630) in a Paris sale room for a
still life of apples by Gauguin. Both men were later rumored to
have been anxious to dispose of large quantities of French francs
before a threatened devaluation of the currency took place. The
previous sale-room record for a Gauguin was, I believe, £17,000
paid a month earlier at Sotheby's for a rather dull work of the
artist's Brittany period. Yet before the year was out the artist's
Tahitian picture *Mao Taporo* realized £64,330 ($180,000) in
New York. And in 1959 *J'Attend Ta Réponse* made £130,000 at
Sotheby's.

The second example was the remarkable case of *La Belle
Strasbourgeoise*, by Nicolas de Largillière, bought by the city of
Strasbourg at Sotheby's in July 1963 for £145,000. The underbidder was a New York dealer presumably acting on behalf of a
client. A year or two before the last war the same picture had
fetched almost exactly one-tenth as much and was for some time
the highest-auction-priced French picture on record. Here, it
seemed clear, was an outstanding instance of the subject matter
of a painting being of paramount importance. It is certainly an
exquisite example of early-eighteenth-century French portraiture,
but had the woman in the picture been wearing fashionable
Parisian clothes of the period instead of the regional costume of
Strasbourg it would probably not have fetched more than £50,000
in 1963. Indeed, Sotheby's anticipated a price of about £45,000.

As is usual after such a surprise boost in price for a minor
master, the sale rooms were suddenly inundated with "Largil-
lières." Most of them were not by Largillière at all; a few were
hack works of the sort that even the best portrait painter turns
out when he is more interested in his fee than in his sitter. It was
not until June 1964, when Christie's were entrusted with the sale
of a group of Largillière portraits of the Throckmorton family,
that the effect of the freak price for *La Belle Strasbourgeoise*
could be seen. Estimates by the pundits of Bond Street (and, ap-

parently, those of Christie's, too) put a top price of £35,000 on a flamboyant portrait of Sir Robert Throckmorton and considerably lower figures on the portraits of his daughter Elizabeth and his aunt Anne, both of whom were painted in nun's habit. The first picture to come up was that of Elizabeth Throckmorton. After a duel which had even the imperturbable Geoffrey Agnew, the most experienced of sale-room duelists, visibly clenching perspiring hands, it was knocked down to Agnew's for 62,000 guineas (Christie's still adhere to this nonexistent coinage, which irritates the buyer but brings in a few—or, as in this case, many thousand—extra shillings). The portrait of Sir Robert was knocked down at 55,000 guineas and the portrait of Aunt Anne at 38,000 guineas. Largillière, who does not rate a single mention in Gerald Reitlinger's compendious history of art prices, *The Economics of Taste*, written in 1960, was confirmed as one of today's fashionable and high-priced artists.

Also in 1964 there was an interesting sequel to the case of *La Belle Strasbourgeoise*, when a second version of the picture, comparable in quality with the first, turned up in the showrooms of Frank Partridge & Sons, exactly opposite Sotheby's in New Bond Street. It had been in the family of Major Edward Baring, of Rye, Sussex, for seventy years, was now offered for sale at only £70,-000. There were no immediate takers. What had happened to the underbidder for the £145,000 picture? Why didn't he jump at the opportunity of getting an equally fine picture of the same subject by the same artist at less than half price? Did the fact that "La Belle" was now no longer unique but had a "twin" make all that difference? We may be fairly certain that had the existence of the second picture been known at the time the first one was sold at Sotheby's, neither version would have been valued at anything like £145,000.

Fashion and rarity, then, both play very important parts in determining the price bracket of a particular artist's work. Both may come about fortuitously, but both can also be engineered. Since, as we have seen, a single phenomenal price may raise the general price level of an artist's entire output, it could be to a dealer's advantage to arrange to buy at an exceptionally high price a single picture by an artist of whose pictures he has a stock. The buying must be done publicly—i.e., at auction, where it may be reported in the press or, at least, will be seen by a large section of the picture-dealing and -buying public. The picture will have been put into the sale, probably under another name, by the dealer, who then bids for it against an accomplice until the right price has been reached. The cost to the dealer will be eight per cent (the trade rate charged by the London auctioneers) of the knock-down price of the picture. If now, instead of throwing his whole stock of the artist's work onto the market, he lets it dribble out slowly, thus creating the impression of scarcity, the gamble may pay off handsomely.

I do not know of any case in which this was done on a really big scale (it would take a Joe Duveen to do it in the grand manner), but there is no doubt that it has been done to boost the prices of certain Victorian artists and some of the minor Impressionists. It has also been used by some dealers to justify the raising of prices for the work of living artists for whom they act as agents. It can be regarded, I suppose, as just another method of publicizing a product, no more reprehensible than any other method and more effective than most.

Publicity of a more orthodox kind has played an increasingly important part during the past few years in the art market. In a radio interview Peter Wilson of Sotheby's said that he did not think that publicity could do anything for an artist's work unless the artist had "got something." From the auctioneer's viewpoint this is probably true, for the sale room is generally a graveyard for the phony. Many a sham artist in the past decade has made quick and easy money out of exhibitions based on publicity gimmicks and little more, but when his pictures reach the sale room their owners get a shock. Sotheby's have themselves made use of publicity to great advantage during the past few years. In an article called "Values Behind the Value" the art critic of the *Daily Telegraph*, Terence Mullaly, wrote that a "potent influence upon prices is exerted by carefully controlled publicity, by the establishment of an aura of prestige around a particular auction room," an obvious allusion to Sotheby's. But the "aura of prestige" surrounding Sotheby's began with the Goldschmidt sale of 1958*— before the firm began to employ publicity men. It was primarily a product of the enterprising way in which Sotheby's took advantage of the removal in 1954 of restrictions on imports from the United States. After the largely unsolicited publicity brought by that sale, interest in art prices (not to be confused with interest in art) suddenly blossomed profusely. It became fashionable to be able to talk about the latest spectacular sale as if it were the latest first night. In the 1760s, Sir Alec Martin tells us, young ladies were warned by fashionable writers that a visit to Christie's was the correct thing to do during the London season. In the 1960s it was Sotheby's turn.

Later in the same article Mr. Mullaly said:

Yet all the time fashion is becoming less important. As more and more objects disappear into museums, never to come out again, and as the number of collectors increases, prices rise, records are inevitably broken every week, and equally inevitably, fashion embraces ever wider fields.

But as more and more pictures disappear into the museums and the number of collectors increases, fashion, surely, becomes all the more important. When the Impressionist and Post-Impressionist gold mines were running out, new gold mines, i.e., new fashion-

* See p. 128.

able artists, had to be created, not only because the dealers had to live but because the wealthy new collectors, most of whom knew little or nothing about painting, wanted to buy what was fashionable. They were given Bonnard, Vuillard, Boudin, Picasso, Braque, and a dozen others, all of whom are already too highly priced for any but the rich to invest in. What the serious collector-investor, especially the one of modest means, needs to know is which of those artists, living or dead, whose works are cheap or moderately priced now will be considerably more fashionable or popular, and therefore in a considerably higher price bracket, in ten, twenty or thirty years' time than they are now. This I shall now foolishly rush in and attempt to tell him.

3

Tomorrow's Winners

> Nowadays people know the price
> of everything and the value of
> nothing.
>
> —OSCAR WILDE,
> *The Picture of Dorian Gray*

> The secret preoccupation of
> many collectors . . . is to ensure
> that a work of art is as good an
> investment as it is attractive to
> look at.
>
> —MAURICE RHEIMS,
> *Art on the Market*

Unlike most tipsters, I propose to take you into my confidence and reveal the method I have used in my prognostications. (In return I shall expect a commission on all profits made as a result of using my list of prospective winners. I do *not* wish to hear from anyone who loses money.) Let us, to begin with, take a quick look at what has happened in the London art market since the last war. What are the most significant things to note? First, and most obvious, the tremendous rise in prices of pictures by the great Impressionist and Post-Impressionist masters and, as the supply of these was seen to be getting thin, the quick follow-up with Picassos, Braques,

Matisses, Bonnards, Vuillards, Utrillos, Vlamincks, Soutines, Modiglianis, etc. Second, the phenomenal prices paid for remnants attributed to the hallowed Renaissance trinity, Leonardo, Michelangelo and Raphael, and for the few paintings outside captivity of such masters as Rembrandt, Hals, Rubens and Goya. Third, the unprecedented scale of investment in the work of contemporary artists. Fourth, the revival of interest (in Britain and America) in the Pre-Raphaelites and other Victorian artists. Fifth, a renewal of admiration for meticulous technique and for those subjects that traditionally go with it—flower pieces, still lifes, genre and anecdote. Sixth, the rise of a new generation of collectors of drawings. Seventh, soaring prices for the pictures of the lone figures among artists of past and present, primitives, eccentrics, visionaries, etc., from Blake, Palmer and Dadd to Alfred Wallis, Stanley Spencer, L. S. Lowry and many so-called "modern primitives."

Now let us look at these points one at a time. How do the Impressionists and Post-Impressionists stand today and how will they stand in the future? It became quite obvious during 1963 and 1964 in the London and New York sale rooms that it is only a shortage of first-class works on the market that has prevented the repeated breaking of records. Some of the prices paid for inferior pictures by the masters of these schools were, in their way, more remarkable than the record prices, and it seems fairly certain that if, for example, the seven pictures in the Goldschmidt sale were to be sold today they would fetch as much as if not more than they did in 1958. Even more certain is that if the choicest major works of these masters were put into the sale room all the present records would be doubled. So far as Cézanne is concerned the point was more than proved in November 1964 when the National Gallery, London, acquired *Les Grandes Baigneuses*, a large but not particularly choice work, for around £500,000 in a private deal. Today Manet's *Bar at the Folies Bergère*, Renoir's *Madame Charpentier and Her Children*, Gauguin's *Ia Orana Maria*—such things as these would all surely realize a quarter of a million pounds or more. And no doubt they will go on increasing in value for many years yet. But in thirty years' time, when the collector has for a long time had his affections transferred to artists whose work is in more plentiful supply, Impressionist and Post-Impressionist pictures in general, having lost all superficial fashionable appeal, will begin to find their true place in the history of art and in the art museums. By then the public will have other idols, television will be showing old films of the lives of Jackson Pollock and Yves Klein instead of Gauguin and Lautrec, and only the sort of people who now look seriously at Delacroix and Turner will have much time for Monet and Cézanne. All the artists will have been sub-jected to review in the light of the stark materialist philosophy of the day (poor old Renoir may even have been temporarily rele-gated to the basement for being too sweet), and for the next forty or fifty years, until they are suddenly rediscovered by another generation, nobody will take much notice of them. But a few smart boys will, of course, have been buying up every remaining scrap of their work they can lay hands on, ready for the great revival of interest in A.D. 2035.

Briefly, then, if you have the right sort of money buy the best Impressionist or Post-Impressionist work you can and you may still expect to make a good profit on it over the next decade or two. But don't hang on to it for more than twenty years unless it is intended as an insurance policy for your great-grandchildren. The same sequence of events will probably ensue in the case of Picasso, Braque, Matisse and company, but the time schedule will be ten years or more behind throughout and it may be your great-great-grandchildren who will benefit.

It is axiomatic that the art of every period is continuously sub-ject to reassessment resulting in neglect or approbation according to the lights of every new age. Today, when Leonardo, Michel-angelo, Raphael are priced above all others, it is hard for us to imagine that it has not always been so and may not continue to be so. It is particularly interesting to note that among the strongest critics of the purchase of the Leonardo cartoon for the nation in 1961 were many artists. It was not a case of sour grapes but a sincere belief that the greatest and most diversified genius of the Renaissance is somewhat overrated in this age as a painter. However this may be, there can be no denying that there is something crazy about the prices paid in the past few years for drawings, usually minute fragments, by these three masters. For example: *Madonna and Child with a Cat,* by Leonardo, 3¼ by 2¾ inches, £19,000 (Sotheby's, 1963); *Ascanius Pulling Aeneas Away from Dido's Bed,* by Michelangelo, 3¾ by 2⅞ inches, £12,500 (Sotheby's, 1964); *The Virgin with the Infant Christ and Saint John the Baptist,* by Raphael, 8¹³⁄₁₆ by 6³⁄₁₆ inches, £32,000 (Sotheby's, 1964). These prices suggest the conclusion we can draw from the second of the points we have noted, namely that drawings by many other great masters, including Rembrandt, whose paintings are virtually unobtainable, are still good investments even at today's prices.

Here it may help to interpolate a general word of advice to those would-be collector-investors who, after any sudden increase in an artist's prices, say, "If only I had bought him last month" (or last year). The time to buy, if one can possibly scrape up the money, is immediately after a jump in price is first noticed, otherwise you will soon be saying the same thing again when another jump in the same artist's prices comes along. Better still, of course, is to know in advance when the first price boost is coming. It may come as the result of a proposed major exhibition of the artist's work or of the publication of a book about him, or (in the case of a living artist) because he has just been taken into the "stable" of an important dealer or been highly praised by an important critic. Usually the first intimation one gets is when two people bid each other up in the sale room far beyond the artist's normal ceiling price. That is the time to go out and buy the artist's work at the old price if you can get it. And if you are quick it is surprising where and how cheaply you may get it.

In November 1963 Christie's sold a picture by the eighteenth-century English marine painter Charles Brooking for a new record price of 5,200 guineas. At the same time a St. James's gallery was offering a comparable picture for £3,000. Four months later, at Sotheby's, an identical picture fetched £14,500 and a similar one made £15,500! Early in 1964 a painting by L. S. Lowry sold at Sotheby's for the then surprisingly high figure of £1,000. A minute's walk away the artist's own agents, the Lefèvre Gallery, were selling comparable pictures for three or four hundred pounds less, and continued to do so for several weeks until another picture, again comparable in size, quality and subject, fetched 1,100 guineas at Christie's. Then the artist's agents raised all his prices in accordance with the sale-room prices. And they have been going up ever since. There was an amusing incident at Sotheby's in the summer of 1964 when a Henry Moore bronze *Family Group* was sold for £6,500. In the middle of the bidding a well-known dealer suddenly got up and hurried from the room. Afterward he explained that he had an identical bronze in his gallery priced at £900 and he had been phoning his partner to hide it quickly! There was a sequel a few months later when a third example of the same *Family Group* fetched £7,350 at Christie's.

Our third point, the unprecedented scale of investment in the work of contemporary artists, would be more accurately described as the unprecedented scale of squandering money on contemporary art, for this is much more a gamble than an investment, a symptom, like the millions "invested" in football pools, of our present somewhat shaky period of prosperity and the get-rich-the-easy-way mentality it has bred. Nearly everyone who spends fifty or a hundred pounds on a picture by an unestablished artist hopes he is backing a winner, but the odds are pretty long. As with most new products that we can buy today—motorcars, furniture, clothes, books, clocks, jewelry and so on—the value of most contemporary pictures drops the moment the buyer takes possession of them. Even in the booming art market of today there is room for only a limited number of artists to be successful, and of this limited number most will sooner or later have to become unsuccessful in order to make room for the new successes. So although the stakes may be low the chances of profitable investment in this field are poor.

At a generous estimate, perhaps one half of one per cent of contemporary painting and sculpture perpetrated and sold today will have any market value at all in thirty years' time. And by far the greater part of that half of one per cent will be valued at less than it is now. We are inclined to think in our arrogance that it was only in the nineteenth century that the great mass of professional artists were bad artists, but it is undoubtedly true of this century, too. The only difference is that today there are vastly more artists than there were then and the problem of picking out the good ones is all that much harder. Not that the good artists are necessarily the ones that, in the short run, are good investments. Modern publicity methods applied to the promotion of art have made it possible for bad artists to get to the top and stay there for many years. Today, for example, we are watching the decline of many slick abstract-expressionist artists whose rise and fall has taken perhaps ten or fifteen years. Anyone who backed them in, say, 1955 and sold out five years later could have made a lot of money. But anyone who was rash enough to buy them at the height of their publicity triumphs bought himself a big bear. (Incidentally, another point about this sort of painting is that much of it will probably not endure *physically* for thirty years.)

The decade we have just passed through has been a bonanza for the exhibitionist artist—the artist who was selling *himself* rather than his work, the "gestural" painter who solicited admiration for the speed with which he could deface a huge canvas, with or without the aid of a bicycle or a paint roller, the painter of "space-creating pictures" which turned out to be simply empty pictures, the painter who aped Jackson Pollock's actions without bothering about his intellect. The exhibitionist has had his day. A few of his works may be preserved in museum vaults as illustrations of that period in which art was thrashing about senselessly before deciding which way to go. The rest will gather dust and become worthless, except as roofing for chicken runs. But what of today's painting and who of today's painters, you are asking, will be prized in the art game during the next few decades? The simple answer is: That and those that the leading dealers decide to handle. No new artist can get very far without a dealer. He may ultimately become big enough to have all the dealers running after him, but in the beginning he will be grateful for any dealer who will take him on. He may be brilliant, unique, a genius, but until a dealer is prepared to show and sell his work the artist is working in a vacuum. This may be tough on artists but it makes life easier for investors, for it restricts the field to those artists whose work is, or will be, shown in the dealers' galleries. It follows, too, that there is a great deal of truth in the saying that an artist is as good as his gallery, and that a knowledge of the dealers is at least as important to the collector-investor as a knowledge of the artists.

Many a serious collector-investor follows a particular dealer rather than particular artists, in the same way that a racing man might follow a trainer over a long period rather than particular horses or jockeys. After all, the established dealers are themselves the shrewdest investors in art. They may make some mistakes, but, like unit trusts* (I am beginning to sound like Mr. Rush), they are able to offset their losses against much larger profits. Thus, for example, those collectors who, before the last war, were

---

* Similar to mutual investment funds in the U.S.

lucky enough to get, and wise enough to take, the advice of Mr. Rex de C. Nan Kivell of the Redfern Gallery in London, found themselves with fortunes on their walls after the war. Mr. Nan Kivell had (and, we may assume, still has) a flair for buying the twenty- and thirty-thousand-pound pictures of today when they were still twenty and thirty pounds apiece. In the early thirties, for instance, he exhibited forty paintings by Soutine and offered them at sixty guineas each. Only two were sold, one of them to a friend who insisted on a guarantee that his money would be refunded if he wanted to return the picture. In November 1964, the gallery sold the last but one of those Soutines to the Tate Gallery for £17,000. More recently collectors (there have been several) who were rich enough and shrewd enough to put themselves in the hands of Marlborough Fine Art ten years ago have shared in that firm's astonishing success. So when we come to list those living artists who are going to make money for us in the future we must look closely at the records of their dealers.

The revival of interest in the Pre-Raphaelites and the Victorians, our fourth point, is especially interesting because it is still new enough for those who missed the bus at the first stage to jump on it now and still be fairly sure of a profitable ride. In 1962 a great deal of surprise was expressed in the newspapers when a group of about thirty Pre-Raphaelite paintings belonging to the composer William Alwyn were sold at Sotheby's. A Burne-Jones, it was reported, had risen in price by 6,000 per cent (from eight guineas to £500) since Mr. Alwyn had bought it in the 1950s. A Ford Madox Brown had gone up 1,360 per cent (from £25 to £340) in the same period. It appeared that Mr. Alwyn had not bought the pictures with investment in mind but because he liked them (some people still do this). He had sold, it was said, because he concluded that Pre-Raphaelite prices were moving up as a result of the increasing interest in Victoriana. In fact the up trend was noted much earlier. Anyone smart enough to have drawn the right conclusion from the sale at Christie's in 1946 of Millais's *The Huguenot* for £2,100 could have made even better investments than Mr. Alwyn's, for it was several years before any other Pre-Raphaelite was accorded a comparable "in" sign. Even as late as 1956, when Ford Madox Brown's *Pretty Baa Lambs* made £560 at Sotheby's, there was still time to get in on the ground floor of some of the other Pre-Raphaelites. But only just. In 1957, when Burne-Jones's *Laus Veneris* and Holman Hunt's *Hireling Shepherd* fetched £3,400 and £2,200, everyone in the trade knew the Pre-Raphaelites were coming back and a scramble for their works began. But because of their painstaking methods of working the Pre-Raphaelites were not very prolific, and so the revival was broadened to include other painstaking Victorians and, finally, almost any Victorian.

Why did it happen? A few years ago I asked this question of Mr. James Laver, the historian of costumes and former keeper of the Department of Engravings, Illustrations and Design at the Victoria and Albert Museum. He replied with what I now call Laver's Law. "I have spent a good part of my life," he said, "in trying to plot the 'gap in appreciation'—that is, the time which must elapse before a discarded style comes into favor again. It seems to be a law of our own minds that we find the art forms of our fathers hideous, the art forms of our grandfathers amusing and those of our great-grandfathers attractive and even beautiful." At that time (it was 1960) I was writing about the craze for Victoriana. Looking back, I see that I said:

It is worth noting, however, that Victorian painting has been left out of this bonanza. There are, of course, buyers for any Pre-Raphaelite pictures that turn up and a steady demand for the better Victorian landscapists. But there are as yet only faint signs of a trend toward the rehabilitation of the Victorian anecdotal paintings that crowded the

Royal Academy summer exhibitions during the second half of the nineteenth century.

Less than two years later the "faint signs" became very strong pointers when, in the sale that included Mr. Alwyn's pictures, the series of five moralizing pictures called *The Road to Ruin*, by that master of Victorian anecdotal painting William Powell Frith, R. A., fetched £7,200. Even allowing for inflation, this was a sensational price compared with the £460 they had fetched in 1919 (although it was very considerably less in real money than the £6,300 paid for them in 1878, the year in which they were painted). This was the signal for a sharp rise in the prices of any piece of Victorian moralizing, sentimentality or whimsy by artists mostly far inferior to Frith.

The implications of Laver's Law are far wider than may at first appear. If every generation is to revive the "art forms" of its great-grandfathers—a hypothesis supported not only by the current revival of taste for the Pre-Raphaelites and the Victorians but also the still newer one for Art Nouveau—then we should now be bracing ourselves for a return of Edwardian "art forms," if any can be found (and you may be sure they will). But much more important for the investor is that, working on Mr. Laver's hypothesis, we may forecast that in, say, seventy-five years' time the "art forms" of today will be returning to favor. The only problem is, what are the "art forms" of today? If I understand Mr. Laver correctly they are those art forms that are popular and fashionable today rather than those that are being created today. In which case it will be, as I have already suggested, the painting of the Impressionists and the Post-Impressionists that is revived by our great-grandchildren. There must, of course, also be some contemporary British artists who will fit the bill, but who are they? Can any of our serious artists be said to be popular in the widest sense, as, say, Landseer was in his day? Obviously not. One does not find reproductions of paintings by Graham Sutherland or Ben Nicholson or Ceri Richards on the walls of suburban British homes. The favorites there are still Sir Alfred Munnings and Sir William Russell Flint (both of whom are higher-priced today than ever before) and two extremely successful corn merchants named Tretchikoff and D'Oyly John for whom God forbid that there should ever be any revival.

Point number five, the renewal of admiration for meticulous technique and for flower pieces, still lifes, genre and anecdotal pictures in this manner, is of course a corollary of the revival of the Pre-Raphaelites and the Victorians. Its effect has been to bring onto the market hordes and hoards of banal Italian, French, Spanish and German pictures of the two decades around 1900, so many of them that several dealers specialize in them and Christie's regularly hold what they call "Cardinal sales" after the jovial and bibulous cardinals who feature in the most sought-after sort of such pictures. And as if this were not bad enough there is a thriving trade in spurious works in this manner produced by skillful academic British painters who usually sign themselves with some Continental-sounding name. Although these "trade pictures," as they are called, cannot be classed as fakes or forgeries—no attempt is made to age them or to assign them to known artists—there is no doubt that many people who buy them foolishly believe them to be period pieces.

The rise of a new generation of collectors of drawings (point number six) was an inevitable result of the all-round rise in the price of paintings. Generally prices for drawings by a particular artist were quick to rise in proportion to those of his paintings, but sometimes there were considerable time lags, and collectors who took advantage of them made excellent investments. What the investor of small means should look for now are such Old Master drawings (if any) as he can afford; drawings by those nineteenth-century artists whose paintings are finding new favor; drawings by living painters and sculptors who have recently made, or soon will be making, reputations through leading dealers.

Finally, let's look at the boom in what I have called "primitives, eccentrics, visionaries, etc." Since Blake, Palmer and Dadd have already been priced out of the reach of all but the rich collector, we must look for others of similar ilk among eighteenth- and nineteenth-century artists. John "Mad" Martin, whose pictures are still reasonably priced, might do for a start, but we shall try to find others. Among the artists of this century, too, we must look for others besides those who are already well established with the dealers. Contemporary "primitives" both of Britain and of France may well be worth attention before too many dealers in London and Paris start muscling in on them. In London, the fact that Tooth's have started to hold regular exhibitions of "primitives" is a very good reason for patronizing the tiny Portal Gallery, which has been specializing in them for some years.

In the lists that follow I give a selection of those artists whose work, it seems to me, will sooner or later increase in price. They do not in any way reflect my own taste. In every case there is a reason behind the choice. Sometimes the reason is a very strong one, at other times it is little more than a hunch. The masters of the École de Paris and the German Expressionists, for example, are included because although their prices may seem to us extremely high already it is generally understood in the art trade that within the next decade they will be as costly as the Impressionists and the Post-Impressionists are today (indeed, Picasso already is). At the other end of the scale, an artist like Dame Ethel Walker is included simply because her prices are at rock bottom and, since she certainly had some talent, her prices must go up if only because they cannot go down. One or two names are given for the very good reason that the artists have recently been given contracts by important dealers. At least one artist is listed because he is very old and his prices are likely to rise abruptly when he dies. A few are minor Old Masters whose prices have risen and will continue to rise as the number of works by major Old Masters available to the market dwindles away to nil. Many are artists who were once more popular than they are now but in whom there has been a marked revival of interest recently. A few are artists of considerable quality whose pictures are rarely seen in this country but are highly rated abroad. There is a list, "Laver's-Law List," of artists who were loved by our great-grandfathers and who (if Laver is right) may be expected to make a reappearance on the market at any time now. This list does not include those, like Lord Leighton and Alma-Tadema, who have already reappeared and are listed according to the prices they fetched in the sale rooms in 1964 and 1965. Finally, there is a "Short List" of artists, mainly abstractionists, who have enjoyed enormous fashionable success in recent years but whose work must now, it seems to me, be treated with caution, if only because of the fickleness of fashion. American readers may be surprised that no mention is made in these lists of the current rages among the Op, Pop, New Realist and so-called Pubist artists of their country. They have been left out because their works so rarely appear in the London sale rooms and because, although they have a considerable influence on British artists, they are still (as we shall see in the next chapter) regarded in Britain with suspicion by all but a very few British collectors.

I have omitted all those great Impressionist and Post-Impressionist masters whose best works, if ever they come onto the market, are priced out of the reach of all but the world's biggest public galleries and private Croesuses. And in order further to curtail the lists I have left out all those Old Masters whose places in the history of art are now firmly assured and whose works are therefore assuredly good investments. In the belief that only an idiot could spend more than thirty thousand pounds ($84,000) on a picture without making a good investment, I have had a ceiling price of that amount in mind. In spite of this I have included Picasso and must therefore warn that you cannot get much of a Picasso painting for less than that sum.* Already discerning buyers discriminate sharply between his important works and his enormous output of trivialities, and the gap between prices for these two different sorts of Picassos is likely to widen when at some distant date a sane assessment of his greatness is made.

There are separate lists for (1) the rich, (2) the well-off, (3) the comfortably off, (4) those making ends meet, (5) the hard-up. The divisions are made on the basis of prices that have been paid, in most cases *at auction,* between 1963 and 1966 for single pictures by the artists named in each group, viz., (1) £10,000 to £30,000, (2) £2,000 to £10,000, (3) £250 to £2,000, (4) £50 to £250, (5) under £50. Unless otherwise stated the reference is to good-quality paintings characteristic of the artist's best-known period or periods. If the amount of money involved sounds a lot, remember that it is not a picture you are buying but an investment, probably the best there is outside the property racket. Borrow from the bank if necessary. Or, if you are buying from a dealer, ask for deferred-payment terms.

In most cases the investment should show a profit within a short period—i.e., anything from twenty-four hours to ten years. This is indicated by an S after the name. An M (for medium term) indicates an investment that, bought in 1966, will be profitable in ten to twenty years' time. An L (for long term) indicates one that should yield a profit in fifty to seventy years. The thirty-year gap between the medium and long terms is a period during which there will, I believe, be a revulsion against most of the things we admire today, and although I shall probably be safely dead by then I am not prepared to make any detailed forecasts about it. Where both S and M are shown after a name it implies that the

---

* See illustration section following page 96.

present popularity of an artist's work is expected to continue well beyond the next ten years. S and L together indicates that an artist's prices are expected to decline after the next ten years but may revive after fifty years or more when his work is "rediscovered" by a later generation. Where all three letters, S, M and L, appear together it means that the artist is as near to being a permanently sound investment as we may hope to find.

1. FOR THE RICH

MODERN
ÉCOLE DE PARIS

Braque (S, M, L)   Picasso (S, M, L)
Matisse (S, M, L)   Soutine (S, M)
Modigliani (S, M)

SURREALISTS

Ernst (S, L)   Miró (pre-1950) (S)

ABSTRACTIONISTS

Brancusi (sculpture) (S, M, L)
Kandinsky (pre-1920) (S, M,   Mondrian (S, M, L)
  L)

INTIMISTS

Bonnard (S)   Vuillard (S)

2. FOR THE WELL-OFF

OLD MASTERS

Nicolas Berchem (S, M, L)   D. Teniers the Younger
A. van Ostade (S, M, L)   (S, M, L)
Roelandt Savery (S, M, L)   Richard Wilson (S, M, L)
                                  Philips Wouwerman (S, M, L)

19TH-CENTURY ENGLISH
William Blake (water colors) (S, M, L)
Richard Dadd (S)

Samuel Palmer (water colors) (S)
D. G. Rossetti (S)
James Ward (S)

19TH-CENTURY FRENCH
Corot (S, M, L)
Daumier (S, M, L)
Delacroix (S, M, L)

Millet (S, M, L)
Rodin (sculpture) (S, M, L)
Rosso (Italian) (sculpture) (S)

MODERN
ÉCOLE DE PARIS
Arp (S)
Balthus (S)
Chagall (S)
Derain (S)
van Dongen (S)
Dufy (S)

Giacometti (paintings and sculpture) (S)
Marquet (S)
Pascin (S)
Rouault (S, M)
Staël (S)
Vlaminck (S)

BRITISH
Francis Bacon (S)
Henry Moore (sculpture) (S, M, L)

Ben Nicholson (S)

EXPRESSIONISTS
Beckmann (S, M)
Jawlensky (S, M)
Kirchner (S, M)
Klee (S, M, L)

Kokoschka (S, M)
Munch (S, M, L)
Nolde (S, M)
Schmidt-Rottluff (S)

FUTURISTS
Balla (S)

Boccioni (S)

ABTRACTIONISTS
Kupka (M)

3. FOR THE COMFORTABLY OFF

18TH- AND 19TH-CENTURY ENGLISH

Alma-Tadema (S)
Ford Madox Brown (S)
Burne-Jones (S)
William Etty (S, M, L)
W. P. Frith (S)
Fuseli (S, M, L)
John Glover (S)
Arthur Hughes (S)
Holman Hunt (S)
J. C. Ibbetson (S, M)
Angelica Kauffmann (S)
Landseer (S)
Lord Leighton (S)
C. R. Leslie (S)

John "Mad" Martin (S)
Millais (S)
Albert Moore (S)
George Morland (S, M, L)
G. W. Mote (S)
Alexander Nasmyth (S, M, L)
Patrick Nasmyth (S, M, L)
S. Pether (S)
David Roberts (S, M)
Rowlandson (water colors)
  (S, M, L)
W. Shayer (S)
James Stark (S)
F. W. Watts (S)

19TH-CENTURY EUROPEAN

Daubigny (S, M)
Diaz (S)
Forain (S and M)
Goenuette (S)
Guillaumin (S, M)
Harpignies (S)
Israels (S, M)

Lépine (S)
Monticelli (S)
Puvis de Chavannes (S, M)
Raffaëlli (S)
Théodore Rousseau (S)
Tissot (S)
Troyon (S)

AMERICAN

R. A. Blakelock (S)
Arthur B. Davies (S)

W. S. Horton (S)
Albert Pinkham Ryder (S, M)

MODERN BRITISH

David Bomberg (S)
William Dobell (S)
Russell Drysdale (S)
Epstein (sculpture) (S)
Gaudier-Brzeska (sculpture)
  (S, M, L)
Barbara Hepworth
  (sculpture) (S)
Josef Herman (S)

Gwen John (S, M)
D. H. Lawrence (S)
L. S. Lowry (S, M)
Henry Moore (drawings and
  small sculptures) (S, M)
Sidney Nolan (S)
Sickert (S, M)
P. W. Steer (S)
Sutherland (S, M)

MODERN EUROPEAN

H.-E. Cross (S)
Gromaire (S)
E. Isabey (S)
M. Kisling (S)
Celso Lagar (S)
A. Lebourg (S)

G. Loiseau (S)
M. Luce (S)
Mané-Katz (S)
Jean Marchand (S)
Permeke (S, M)
Mario Sironi (S)

4. FOR THOSE MAKING ENDS MEET

19TH- AND 20TH-CENTURY BRITISH AND EUROPEAN

J. E. Blanche (S)
Martin Bloch (S)
Frank Boggs (American) (S)
Frank Brangwyn (S)
Fred Brown (S)
D. Y. Cameron (S)
George Clausen (S)
T. Sidney Cooper (S, M)
Frank Dobson (sculpture) (S)
Mark Fisher (S)
Charles Furse (S)
Gaudier-Brzeska (drawings)
  (S, M)

W. G. de Glehn (S)
Duncan Grant (S)
Atkinson Grimshaw (S)
David Jones (S)
Peter Lanyon (S)
John Lavery (S)
Maurice Lévis (S)
Ambrose McEvoy (S)
Henry Moore, R.A. (19th cent.)
  (S)
C. R. W. Nevinson (S)
William Nicholson (S)
Orpen (S)

Charles Ricketts (S)   Ruskin Spear (S)
William Roberts (S)   W. Clarkson Stanfield (S, M)
Charles Shannon (S)   Philip Sutton (S)
Sickert (drawings) (S, M)   Henry Tonks (S)
F. N. Souza (S)   Keith Vaughan (S)

5. FOR THE HARD-UP

Most (but not all) of the following are artists whose auction prices showed signs of improvement during 1964–65 after having been at rock bottom. Many of them are still so low-priced that it must be almost impossible to lose money on them. All are suggested as short-term flutters.

H. B. Brabazon (water colors)   Alphonse Legros
Vanessa Bell   Thérèse Lessore
Frank Brangwyn (drawings)   Paul Maitland
John Bratby   Ambrose McEvoy (water colors)
Prunella Clough   Paul Maze (pastels)
Robert Colquhoun   Bernard Meninsky (drawings)
Philip Connard   Winifred Nicholson
Frank Dobson (drawings)   Alfred Parsons
R. O. Dunlop   Adrian Peppercorn
Eric Gill (drawings)   Charles Sims
Albert Goodwin   Jack Smith
Sylvia Gosse   Ethel Walker
Henry Lamb

LAVER'S-LAW LIST

The following are some of those artists who, according to Laver's Law (see page 48), are due (or overdue) for revival about now.

Since it is unlikely that anything can be done to stop this thing happening, a profitable short-term gamble on it seems the best course to take.

Benjamin-Constant	Willem Geest
de Blaas	Frederick Goodall
Rosa Bonheur	Sir James Guthrie
Bouguereau	A. E. Hébert
Jules Breton	Frank Holl
Briton Rivière	E. A. Hornel
John Collier	H. H. La Thangue
A. Delug	Edwin Long
Luke Fildes	Maris brothers
Walther Firle	Willy Martens
P. H. Flandrin	H. W. Mesdag
Fred Morgan	Annie Louisa Swynnerton
W. J. Müller	Eugène Trigoulet
Max Nonnenbruch	W. Trübner
Sir Edward Poynter	Fritz von Uhde
Solomon J. Solomon	Wilhelm Volz
Edward Stott	Frederick Walker
Franz Stück	G. F. Watts

SHORT LIST

The following artists have all had lions' shares of fashionable success during the past decade. But, fashion being what it is, they should, in my opinion, be bought now for love rather than investment.

Pietro Annigoni	Serge Poliakoff
Bernard Buffet	Jean-Paul Riopelle
Georges Mathieu	Pierre Soulages

In reading through those lists you have probably noticed the conspicuous absence of several names that you expected to find there. In most cases the reason for the omission of a particular artist is likely to be that little or none of his work has appeared in the London sale rooms during the period reviewed. In a few cases, however, the reason is that, although an artist's work has featured prominently in the market, it has not been possible to discern any definite "price pattern." The most obvious example of this is Augustus John. Although his work was notoriously inconsistent in quality, that alone does not explain the extraordinary variations in prices paid for his work since his death in 1961.

Competition between top dealers, notably Agnew's and Tooth's, has maintained good prices for the best of John's paintings and drawings (especially where the subjects are the members of his family), although the record price for a drawing is still the £3,800 paid by Agnew's in 1961 and that for a painting is the £8,925 given by Lord Cowdray for a self-portrait in 1962. But prices for all but the choicest works slumped drastically at the second of the artist's studio sales in June 1963. Most of the drawings went for well under £100, and few of the paintings made more than £300. In 1964 the illogicality of the market was typified in a sale at Sotheby's when two paintings that had fetched £252 and £63 a year earlier at Christie's made £120 and £150 respectively, and a third that had sold for £525 at Christie's in 1962 made £150. As an investment the lovable old gypsy looks now, in 1966, as shaky as the drawings of his last years. And as the affection that is felt for him as a character slowly dies, there will, I think, be many shocks for those who bought his work at the peak prices of 1962. John's position in British art was comparable with that of Noël Coward in British theater. With few exceptions the works of both will, I believe, continue to be admired only for as long as their creators' contemporaries are still with us. The same thing is true to some extent of Munnings and Russell Flint, whose works are already so overpriced that I find it difficult to believe that they can be more than very-short-term investments, and I have therefore omitted them.

Before leaving the subject of the lists perhaps it should be said that no magic quality is claimed for them. It is not suggested that you should rush out and buy works by any or all of these artists indiscriminately. I must repeat that all I have tried to do is to name as many as I can of those artists whose work is now (in 1966) evidently appreciating in value or appears likely to appreciate in value at some time in the foreseeable future. Obviously the rate of profit-making will vary enormously from artist to artist. In some cases it may be slow but very sure, in others meteoric but shaky. The would-be investor must explore the market for himself and choose carefully the few artists he fancies putting his money on. Having done that, he should concentrate on these few to the exclusion of all others.

Finally, he must remember that, since the lists were compiled on the basis of *auction* prices, anything he buys from a dealer is likely to take considerably longer to show a profit. But in the early stages of the game this is a fair price to pay for the protection it will give him from the snares and pitfalls that await the innocent in the sale rooms.

4

American Winners?

> *European painting is studied and
> tired, missing the freshness of
> spring. American painting bursts
> forth from the ground like flowers,
> disengaged from tradition and the
> past. If a man moves by plane
> rather than oxcart, why must he
> prefer Rubens to Pollock?*
> —PHILIPPE DOTREMONT,
>   quoted in *Time*, August 11, 1961

> *Prosperity crowns those who
> ride the waves of fashion with a
> timing nice enough to slip from
> one to another before each breaks.*
> —JOHN I. H. BAUR,
> Associate Director,
> Whitney Museum of American Art

As a European collector, M. Philippe Dotremont, the Belgian
industrialist, is a rarity. His attitude to contemporary American
art is shared by few collectors on his side of the Atlantic. While
artists in Europe may readily acknowledge the importance of the
American art revolution of the past decade or two, those Eu-
ropeans who back their beliefs in art with money are much slower
to be convinced. This has little, if anything, to do with chauvinism
(although some French collectors may still be buying the work
of moribund French artists for patriotic reasons). It is primarily

62

a matter of Old World conservatism coupled with the popularly held opinion that all Americans are crazy anyway.

Even after several years of domination of European painting by American painting, most European—and especially British—collectors (and dealers too) still nurse the idea that the "new American painting" is a flash in the pan. They are suspicious of the way in which art is promoted in the United States and are unable to free themselves of the erroneous conviction that only cheap-Jack products are sold by cheap-Jack methods. For the most part their attitude to their American counterparts is that of indulgent parents to wayward children. They smile a superior smile and think, "Let them get on with it. They'll learn in time."

In the autumn of 1965, the superior smile became a guffaw when *Life International* magazine featured Mr. and Mrs. Robert C. Scull in an article on Pop art headed "If You Buy It, How Do You Live with It?" The illustrations showed Mr. Scull apparently breakfasting on grapefruit and *vin rosé* while seated against a background of a highly indigestible 16-foot painting by James Rosenquist, and Mr. and Mrs. Scull posing like gourmets in front of a Claes Oldenburg stove laden with painted plaster food. The text quoted Mr. Scull as saying that when he bought the Rosenquist in 1962 for $1,400 the artist stood and looked at him in astonishment and then said, "I didn't think there'd be anyone crazy enough to buy it."

Rosenquist's opinion of Scull's sanity must have been shared by the great majority of those who read that article, but later events have suggested that businessman Scull is likely to have the laugh on us all. In order to make room in his life for his increasing collection of Pop works (including a second Rosenquist, 85 feet long and $60,000 high) he had to dispose of thirteen paintings by De Kooning, Kline, Newman, Rothko, Still and other contemporary American artists of a generation senior to the Pop boys. It was these pictures that came up for sale at the Parke-Bernet Galleries on October 13, 1965.

The catalogue of this sale was a monument to Mr. Scull's far-sightedness as a collector-investor. In almost every case the entries pertaining to his pictures included lists of impressive exhibitions to which the pictures had been lent. It would be invidious to suggest that in generously lending his treasured possessions to public exhibitions Mr. Scull was influenced by the fact that it would add to their value when he came to sell them. But the fact remains that it did just that. Significantly, the most exhibited work in the sale, Willem de Kooning's *Police Gazette,* made the highest price, $37,000. A Clyfford Still made $29,000, a Newman $26,000 and a Mark Tobey $14,000. But, viewed from London, the most remarkable price of the sale was $20,000 for Robert Rauschenberg's chaotic combine painting *Express.* This picture was not from the Scull collection, but its price must have given Mr. Scull high hopes of the investment prospects of the pictures he still had at home.

But what exactly are those prospects? Two other New York Pop-art collectors, interviewed by *Life,* gave diametrically opposite views. Mr. Leon Kraushar, who owns one of Tom Wesselman's *Great American Nude* series,* a stack of Andy Warhol's Brillo boxes and Claes Oldenburg's *Big Baked Potato,*† holds that "Pop is the art of today, and tomorrow, and all the future." All other art, he says, is for old ladies, but Pop pictures "are like IBM stock and this is the time to buy, because Pop is never going to die." But Mr. Harry Abrams is more realistic. When he buys a Pop picture it has to be good enough to stand up to competition from his Monet, Modigliani, Chagall and Picasso. And he has no illusions about the ephemeral nature of most Pop. Of the Pop artists he says, "They're giving us a new way to look at things, to

---

* See illustration section following page 96.

† See illustration section following page 96.

notice what's around us. They may even be changing our whole idea of what taste is. *Before we know it, they'll be the old ones and we'll be on to something else . . .*"

In Britain, where money is shorter, this more wary attitude to the latest art kick prevails over all others. What Americans call their "Vanguard Audience" has only a very feeble counterpart in Britain. Conditioned for so long to the idea that France was the birthplace of all modern art and would continue to be so forever and ever, the British find it almost impossible to believe even in their own modern artists until (as in the cases of Henry Moore and Francis Bacon) they are acclaimed by other countries. It is hardly surprising, then, that such manifestations of the great American art revolution as have appeared in the London sale rooms during the past few years have called forth little covetousness in the bosoms of British collectors and that prices have been low. In December 1962 a De Kooning approximately the same size as one that made $24,000 for Mr. Scull fetched only £650 ($1,820) at Sotheby's. In the same sale a Clyfford Still, smaller but comparable in quality with the $29,000 canvas in the Scull collection, made £3,600 ($10,000). In 1963, a Mark Tobey tempera painting comparable in size, quality and date with the $14,000 one sold at Parke-Bernet went for £1,575 ($4,410) at Christie's.

For a time it was possible for the collector of the new American painting to snap up a few bargains in London sale rooms, but by the winter of 1965 the supply of such works had almost completely dried up. Following the success of works of this category in the sales, at Parke-Bernet, of the Ira Haupt collection in January 1965 and the Dotremont collection in April of the same year (a Pollock of 1946 made $44,000, a De Kooning of 1959 $40,000, a Gottlieb of 1959 $12,000, a Sam Francis of 1954 $16,500 and a Guston of 1957 $10,000) no vendor in his right senses was likely to send modern American paintings of any importance to Sotheby's or Christie's. And up to the time of writing (early 1966) not a single example of American Pop art (unless we count Larry Rivers as a Pop artist) has, so far as I am aware, come up for auction in London.

What are regarded in Britain as the ridiculously high prices charged by American dealers for modern American paintings must also have militated against the collection of such works in Britain. Not even Marlborough Fine Art, with its New York "branch," the Marlborough-Gerson Gallery, has made any serious attempt to convert the British collector to contemporary American art, while the gallant Kasmin Gallery, which has been devoted to propagating its soberer manifestations, has found the crusade extremely hard going. But it is not only the big price that alienates the Briton. He does not like the big format either. He equates it with the boastfulness and ostentatiousness of what he believes is the typical American, a big man with a big cigar in his big mouth, riding in an absurdly big automobile. There is also a much deeper reason. The British are not yet fully converted to the American craving for the new. It will come, of course, as every bad American influence—from commercial television to drug taking and from Woolworth's oil paintings to sex mania—has come. With increased affluence we too shall embrace the trade-it-in-throw-it-away philosophy which keeps the wheels of the United States' never-never economy turning. We are already well on the way to believing, with our American cousins, that we must have the newest-model motorcar, television, refrigerator and washing machine, so why not the newest-model art? Is not the only difference that, whereas the discarded motorcar, television set or washing machine has lost most if not all of its original value, the discarded painting may, as we have seen in the case of Mr. Scull, prove to have increased in value? As a status symbol, then, new art has this special advantage over other status symbols. But how has it acquired this special advantage?

In the past art collectors who spent large sums of money were usually cautious about the new. They waited for the worth of new developments in art to be assessed by the critics and proven by time. Now, if we are to believe American art critic Harold Rosenberg (and we are!), newness itself has a big price tag. In his essay "The New as Value"* he describes how this has come about. "Novelties in painting and sculpture receive notice in the press as new *facts*," he says, "long before they have qualified as new *art*." Once sufficient public attention has been drawn, by whatever means, to a novel work, the critics are bound to take notice of it. And not only to take notice of it, but to approve of it, because "to deny the significance of the new product begins to seem futile, since whatever is seen and talked about is already on its way to becoming a *fait accompli* of taste." From there the work will be "nudged into art history" and "through attaining this place the work's own qualities become part of the standards by which the work is judged."

I am reminded, by this description of the farce to which art in America has descended, of the hoaxer who, in my youth, delivered a lecture to a learned society on "the new philosophy, in which effect precedes cause." But the situation in American art is no short-term joke. Huge sums of money (not to mention many huge reputations) are staked upon its enduring for a long time. You may feel that the whole damn lot should be dumped into Central Park and burned, but this has nothing to do with the purpose of this chapter, which is to attempt to estimate how long the farce will go on and to advise the investor which players in the farce are the best for him to put his money on.

There was a time when the inclusion of an artist's work in the permanent collections of great museums of modern art made that artist a fairly safe bet for the collector. But the processes by which so many of such works now find their way into those museums has

---

* Included in his book *The Anxious Object*.

made this guarantee virtually worthless. Describing these processes, Mr. Rosenberg says that

reputations are now being made in art as fast as on Broadway and in Hollywood. The past few seasons have provided the spectacle of museum personnel, critics and professors of current art history being swept up in a race to identify themselves with half-emerged personalities and trends; curators touring the country as advance agents for exhibitions of neo-this or that; public and private buyers acquiring collections that amount to kits made up of the latest names; university instructors playing the part of sideshow barkers in front of the slides flipped through their projection machines . . . The speed-up in history-making has now reached the point where the interval of critical evaluation seems to have become superfluous.*

I was once told by the director of a great museum of modern art that his job was not to create a collection of good or great art but only to make sure that the collection reflected what was going on in art. Now even that aim has been abandoned by many people in positions such as his, especially in America. Lack of conviction that much of the art of today is, in fact, art at all has forced them to leave such judgment to posterity. But for the private investor-collector this is not good enough.

Most museum basements are stacked with works that were once highly prized, are now despised but may one day make at least a partial comeback. Most of the abstract-expressionist, Pop and Op art that has found its way into American museums in recent years will be subject to this appreciation-contempt-reappraisal cycle. How long it will take can be only guesswork, but the reassessment will be made long after the blare of publicity that accompanied the work's first showing has died away. It will be made on the basis of the part the work played in the evolution or

---

* Harold Rosenberg, *op. cit.*

development of the "school" to which it belongs. Even so, it will
not be a wholly objective judgment, because the judges will be
raring to apotheosize some homebred masters. For, although
M. Philippe Dotremont sees the disengagement from tradition
of modern American painting as a virtue, American art pundits so
hunger after a tradition they can call their own that they will in-
vent one if necessary.

Already it is clear that numbered among the gods created in
this way will be Jackson Pollock, Mark Rothko, Willem de Kooning and Franz Kline, with, on a slightly lower deific level, Hans
Hofmann, Adolph Gottlieb, Arshile Gorky, Mark Tobey, Barnett
Newman, Clyfford Still and, perhaps, Robert Motherwell. Then
hovering like *putti* around these gods will be such artists as Morris
Louis, Fritz Glarner, David Smith, Baziotes, Sam Francis, Ells-
worth Kelly, Noland and Guston. In spite of the high prices that
must already be paid for the work of most of these artists, they
are probably still good short-term investments, and the best of
them should pay off in the long run too. But do not be surprised
if they flag a bit in the middle distance, because, before they are
finally pigeonholed as twentieth-century "old masters" (along
with Marin, Stuart Davis, Joseph Stella, Arthur Dove, etc.) there
will be a period in which the believers in art-for-newness'-sake
will rate them old-fashioned.

Agreed that these leaders of various brands of abstract art are
already assured places in art's vast heaven, what of the later gen-
erations, the Pop men and after? There is already ample evidence
that some of them are good short-term investments. Rauschenberg, for example, must surely have made money for whoever sold
his *Express* of 1963 for $20,000 in 1965. But will the thing last?
How long, for instance, can Andy Warhol's silk-screened Brillo
cartons retain the "magic" that makes them worth $300 or more
apiece to members of the American Vanguard Audience? One
answer is: much longer than the Pop haters think. For Pop has

already lasted long enough to make a few paragraphs in the history books, and those Brillo cartons that survive long enough may well become treasured exhibits in museums of anthropology, the manifestations of a mad period in which the more the artists railed against the old art values and thumbed their noses at the collectors and experts, the wider those collectors and experts spread their arms to receive the material expressions of their abuse. And paid big money for the privilege of doing so. In such an opportunist's heaven it is almost too much to expect any artist to keep his integrity, and definitely too much to expect to find any great art.

The investment value of Pop has nothing to do with whether it is great art, or whether it is art at all. It has to do only with how long the fad (the word is Warhol's, not mine) can go on. And that is until the next fads (Op and pornography?) have completely eclipsed it, or until the inevitable economic crisis teaches the rich to be more discriminating. Until then, go ahead and buy yourself a Warhol Brillo carton or some of Oldenburg's plaster food, a Jasper Johns beer can or a Jim Dine toaster. But don't try to sell them in Britain. The British cannot be persuaded to take art lightly, still less to pay for lightweight art.

Oh, and don't try to sell your precious Andrew Wyeths here, either. We have scores of equally finicky, sentimental paintings in the basement store at the Tate Gallery. Most of them were painted about a hundred years ago. It is absurd that a painter who, stylistically at least, really belongs to the nineteenth century should be the highest-priced American artist in the third quarter of the twentieth century, and I would not, therefore, like to risk any of my money on his chances of remaining in the same position in the fourth quarter. The Americans' admiration for the "loner" in art would be better applied to Ben Shahn.

5

Snares
and
Pitfalls

The position of a man in our society who would like to discover a real work of art among the mass of material that pretends to be art is like that of a man walking along a riverbank sown with a mosaic of artificial stones, looking for the single diamond, ruby or topaz that he reckons he can find among all these thousands of glistening fakes.
—LEO TOLSTOY,
"What Is Art?"

Once upon a time, when I was more innocent than I am now, I was surprised to see several paintings by minor Impressionist masters in one of London's smaller auction rooms. Scenting a bargain, I decided to have a go at one of them and selected a well-painted canvas catalogued as "Luce—*Barges on the Seine*." I calculated that if it was by Maximilien Luce (and it seemed to me that it was) it would be worth three or four hundred pounds, but at this sale room, in which I had already made one or two very good buys, it might easily go for very much less. It had to if I was to get it.

On the day of the sale I was among the first arrivals in the auction room. I examined every new arrival, hoping all the time that I would not see any of the bigger dealers. By the time the sale began there were about forty people present and only one of them was known to me as a dealer, a man who had never been known to spend more than twenty pounds on any lot. My hopes rose and the half hour before my lot (I was already thinking of it like that) seemed interminable. Then, suddenly, the auctioneer was saying, "Lot So-and-so. Five pounds, anybody?" Nobody lifted a finger or batted an eyelid. "Two pounds, then?" he said, and added immediately, "Two pounds I'm bid."

The bidding rose a pound at a time to twenty pounds, by which time I had noticed that one of the two bidders was a member of the auctioneers' staff who was frequently entrusted by dealers to bid for them in their absence. This I interpreted as meaning that a dealer, probably an expert on the work of Luce, confirmed my opinion of the picture. This was flattering but disappointing as well, because the dealer was sure to be prepared to pay more than I was. As these thoughts passed through my mind the bidding stopped at twenty-eight pounds in favor of the staff man.

"Sold at twenty-eight pounds, then," said the auctioneer, looking around the room hopefully. I waved my catalogue. "Thirty pounds. Thirty pounds at the back of the room. Against you in front. Thirty pounds." He brought down his little gavel, bang! and the picture was mine. But immediately I began to have misgivings. At the moment of victory comes the chastening thought that one has paid more than anyone else in the room was prepared to pay and that, therefore, one has paid too much. Even the experienced dealer often has this feeling, but it usually passes quickly. For me it was not a case of having paid too much but of having paid too little. The moment the picture was knocked down to me I knew I had boobed. At that price it could not (in spite of the bold signature in the right-hand corner) be a genuine

Luce or the dealer, for whom I was convinced the staff man was bidding, would not have dropped out at thirty pounds.

After the sale I told a dealer friend what I had done. "Oh dear," he said. "If that picture is by Luce I'm Vincent van Gogh." Well, without even looking at him I knew he was not Vincent van Gogh, so I tucked my tail between my legs and went home. I was very angry with myself, but I had learned a good lesson, which, it occurred to me, I ought to impart to the readers of a column I was then writing in an art magazine. With this in mind I telephoned the auctioneers to ask for more information about the "Luce" and the other "Impressionist" pictures in the sale. One outcome of this conversation was that the next day I received a letter which is, I think, worth quoting here in full:

Dear Mr. Wraight,

I was so intrigued and puzzled by a remark you made during our telephone conversation that I cannot resist writing to you, if not to advise you, at least to put you right regarding an aspect of cataloguing which I think you do not perhaps quite understand. The pictures offered in yesterday's sale were quite openly disclosed as being extremely doubtful works. The Delacroix was given as "bears signature"; you may or may not know that there is a distinct difference between this and the statement of fact that a piece is signed. The name of Luce was given without initials but with the qualification that the work *was* signed; this implies that although I thought the signature was genuine, I took the work itself to be doubtful, although of excellent quality. It has long been the habit of French painters to sign the works of students or followers—Corot, in particular, made a great practice of this; it was merely a master's sign of favour to a promising pupil or follower. Henry [sic] Martin was catalogued as merely bearing monogram, Lot 47, quite distinctly signed with a famous name, was catalogued merely as "19th Century (bears signature)," Lot 48 is merely attributed to Guillamin [sic], the remarks referring to Lot 47 also refer to Lot 49, and Lot 50, indisputably Fritz Martin, was clearly marked as signed and inscribed. What further guidance does any sensible buyer want, other than bold letters printed across the catalogue, "This is a Fake"?

It would seem to me that most private individuals interested in paintings and buying in salerooms harbour the fond hope that they know a little more than Auctioneers or their staff, and that through this they will buy an extremely good picture cheaply. I have yet to hear such a man complaining because he has made a lot of money out of such a find, but they are always ready to say that Auctioneers, or their clients the vendors, have been unfair if they are forced, through competition, to pay a fairly high price for a picture. It is fairly obvious that a good "School" picture will always make a high price, so long as there are arty-crafty shops in the suburbs serving arty-crafty customers anxious to have pictures that look something like a Luce, a Corot or even a Matisse.

To anyone unaccustomed to the art game this must seem a remarkable, even an alarming, letter full of a curious sort of double talk. In fact it contains a lot of valuable information, not only about the danger of encountering fakes and forgeries in the sale room, a subject to which we shall return in a later chapter, but also about what I call catalogue codes. These codes, or methods of cataloguing, may vary considerably from sale room to sale room, and an understanding of them is essential to the tyro who cannot afford to learn through bitter experience.

From the letter I have quoted above you might get the impression that fine-art auctioneers do not encourage private individuals to buy in the sale room. This is, of course, wrong. An increasingly large proportion of sales is being made to private buyers, and their business is almost as important as that of the dealers. Yet after talking to many of these private buyers, especially at sales of "old masters," I have come to the conclusion that very few of them understand the catalogues they have in their hands. And there is often little to help them in those catalogues except a clause in the "conditions of sale" that goes something like this:

"The auctioneers are not responsible for errors of description, or for the genuineness or authenticity of any lot, or for any fault or defect in it."

Some auctioneers cover themselves further with a clause that says: "All pictures are by, after or in the manner of the artist named." But, naturally, in the big auction houses, where there are experts on the staff, considerable effort is made to determine which the picture is—"by," "after" or "in the manner of." The findings of these experts are then made known in the catalogue by means of the "code," which at Sotheby's and Christie's is virtually the same.

Perhaps I can best illustrate how it works by recalling a conversation I heard during an Old Master sale at Sotheby's. An attractive full-length portrait of a child, catalogued as "Rubens," had just been sold for £490 when a woman remarked to a dealer sitting beside her, "That was a cheap Rubens."

"That's because it wasn't a Rubens," said the dealer.

"What d'you mean?" she asked, pointing to her catalogue. "It says here 'Rubens.'"

"Exactly," replied the dealer. "That simply means it is in the manner of Rubens or perhaps a copy of a Rubens. If Sotheby's believed it was really by Rubens it would say 'Sir Peter Paul Rubens.' If they thought it was not by him but was perhaps from his workshop they would probably write 'Sir P. P. Rubens.'"

Rubens was not, perhaps, the best example to take to illustrate the point, since his mass-production methods make his *œuvre* the most disputed of all. He regarded all the pictures painted in his studio as his own and would argue that studio replicas were not mere copies—"they are so skilfully retouched by my own brush that they are virtually indistinguishable from the originals." And he would add that they had the great advantage of being cheaper. Still, insofar as the different ways of giving his name in catalogues indicate the assessment by the auctioneers' experts of the degree of authenticity of the particular pictures, Rubens will do. Similar variants can be made of almost any artist's name—Lawrence, Sir T. Lawrence, Sir Thomas Lawrence, P.R.A.; Morland, G. Morland, George Morland; Ostade, A. van Ostade, Adriaen van Ostade, and so on. Sometimes, notably in the cases of fathers and sons of the same names, four variants may be found, as, for example, Teniers, D. Teniers, David Teniers the Younger (or Elder).

Where cataloguing is done in this way it means that the buyer gets not only a picture but also an expert opinion on it. Experts, however, are by no means infallible, even at Sotheby's and Christie's. But a mistake in a catalogue can never fool all the dealers all the time. Often at a sale one sees them bidding furiously against each other for some apparently unimportant picture that they alone realize is by a much more important artist than the one named in the catalogue. At Christie's, not so long ago, I sat next to a friend who is a collector of English water colors, and was very surprised when he bid to 600 guineas for a water color of a rather dull architectural subject, catalogued as by "Turner of Oxford" (William Turner). While he was explaining to me that it was in fact by J. M. W. Turner, it was sold at 1,300 guineas. At Sotheby's in November 1963 two very fine views of Rome, catalogued as the work of Bernardo Bellotto, were sold for £30,000 and £17,000. A few months later, when one of them was destroyed in a fire at a West End dealer's, they were described as by Canaletto, who was Bellotto's uncle and his master. There was no question here of the dealer having "upgraded" them in order to increase their value. Even during his lifetime Bellotto was mistaken for his famous uncle, whom he is said to have impersonated at times to his own advantage. He was, however, a very fine painter in his own right and today his pictures can be almost as highly priced as Canaletto's. In this particular case it would probably have been to the dealer's advantage if the pictures had been Bellottos. Then both would probably be still in existence and one would probably be in the National Gallery, for, shortly after the sale at Sotheby's, Sir Philip Hendy, director of the National Gallery, had called on the dealer in the hope of finding a Bellotto for the Gallery's collection. Had he not agreed with the dealer's attribution to Canaletto both pictures would, at the time of the fire, have been at the National Gallery for inspection by the trustees. In the long run the reputations of fine-art auctioneers must largely depend upon the scholarship put into the preparation of their catalogues. There are, however, several sale rooms that handle a large volume of picture business without employing any experts, and it is probably at their sales that the knowledgeable collector stands the best chance of making a find. They are also wonderful places for the unknowledgeable to make mistakes. If any and every picture that looks vaguely like a Turner, for instance, is catalogued in the same way, the chances are that nine hundred and ninety-nine out of a thousand of them are not by Turner and that only an expert will recognize the one that is.

The vastness of the problem of wrong attributions is not generally realized outside the art trade, but anyone who, as I am, is always at sales in town and country has only to be able to count to realize that such artists as John Constable and David Cox, for example, would have had to live five hundred years to have painted all the pictures accredited to them. When I first began to go to sales in the country, especially those held in undistinguished houses, I was amazed at the sums paid for worthless pictures. On one occasion, after receiving a catalogue that listed water colors by John Constable, Peter de Wint, Patrick Nasmyth and others, I went to view the contents of a private house. Nearly all the pictures were amateurish daubs in water color, some bearing famous names but the majority signed with the name of the recently deceased owner of the house. It needed no Maigret to deduce that all these water colors were by the same "artist," for she had made no attempt to imitate the masters' styles but had simply copied their subjects. Yet the "Nasmyth" and the "de Wint" each fetched over twenty pounds, while her own "originals" fetched a few shillings. Bidding for the "Constable," which made £32, was interrupted about halfway through when someone called out, "Is it really by Constable?" and the auctioneer shot back, "Well, it's got his name on it!"

I have often wondered what the buyers of those things think they have got and whether the belief that they have a Constable or a Nasmyth or a de Wint at bargain prices is not all they want —whether they would, in fact, get any more pleasure from the real thing. Today, more than ever before, it's the name that counts. But buying "names," unless you are prepared and able to pay the market price for them, may easily prove a finger-burning business. As we shall see in the next chapter, only a minority of wrongly attributed pictures are deliberate fakes. A large proportion of them are copies or imitations made, in all innocence, by the thousands of nineteenth-century amateurs who amused themselves in that way before the days of mass entertainment, cinema, radio and television. By adding signatures to the better examples of these amateur efforts, certain gentlemen whose only artistic accomplishment is that they can write "Corot" or "Constable," etc., are making a comfortable little living out of the gullible without any of the laborious business of actually painting or drawing anything.

If you are thinking of spending any appreciable sum on a painting at a sale, give all the time you can to finding out exactly what it is you are going to buy. View the picture on the first possible occasion and use the rest of the time before the sale to ask questions about it and look up reference books. Even where you are quite happy about a picture's authenticity do it just the same. The sale rooms are the best free universities there are for an education in the art game, and the knowledge you gain there over the years will be invaluable.

6

Forgeries,
Fakes
and
Fiddles

> A kind of university exists for
> the training of forgers. It is kept
> going by the stupidity of
> purchasers.
>
> —AUGUSTO JANDOLO,
> Confessions

During one week in 1961 I saw a play about the Dutch forger
Han van Meegeren, reviewed a new book about art forgeries and
wrote a short article* about an exhibition called "Forgeries and
Deceptive Copies" which was held at the British Museum. For
reasons I will explain later I repeat that article here:

Forgery, always a fascinating subject, seems now to be more fascinating than ever to the layman. On the day that I went to the exhibition the crowds round the showcases were so dense I had to fight my

---

* In *The Tatler*, February 22, 1961.

way in to get a glimpse of the unicorn's horn (lent by Sir Kenneth Clark) and the mummified mermaid, both dating from the seventeenth century, or of the phony flint axes, produced by "Flint Jack" around 1860, and the falsified fossils originally intended, by the students who made them, simply as a joke on a professor.

The exhibition extends far beyond the field of the graphic arts. The activities of forgers and copyists in the realms of natural history, ethnography, manuscripts, music, postage stamps and numismatics are all illustrated extensively. Antiquities are divided under the headings Greek and Roman, Egyptian and Western Asiatic, Medieval and Later, and Oriental. Fake antique furniture is a conspicuous absentee—but there is a modern Chinese fake of an eighteenth-century English clock, complete with a spurious, but cunningly unreadable, maker's signature.

Among the pictures and sculptures are the echoes of some fine scandals. A group of imitation Corots recalls the crack that "of 3,000 pictures painted by Corot, 10,000 are now in America." An oil painting in the style of an old Dutch master commemorates the sensational career of van Meegeren.

No less intriguing than the van Meegeren story is that of Peter Thompson, a large selection of whose antiquarian and topographical drawings are on show. Whereas the Dutchman invented merely a new "period" for Vermeer, Thompson invented an entirely new artist. He called his creation "Captain John Eyre" and gave him not only an œuvre, but also a complete and complex life history and character.

Thompson, who lived and worked in London around the middle of last century, was a carpenter and builder with some small talent for drawing architectural subjects. In turning to the faking of old drawings he seems to have been prompted by some idea of getting his own back on the government, at whose hands he claimed to have suffered "a severe loss."

That he was no fool is plain from the fact that he made "Captain Eyre" an amateur artist, thereby explaining the weakness of his drawings, which, since they purported to have been made in the first half of the seventeenth century, were of historical rather than artistic interest.

He gave Captain Eyre a precise birth date, October 6, 1604, and a pedigree. He made him a descendant of a famous Lord Mayor of London and endowed him with a distinguished military record in the service of both the Royalists and the Parliamentarians.

His enthusiasm and ambition for the Captain were enormous and no doubt led to his ultimate undoing. The drawings were usually elaborately annotated. On one the "artist" wrote a long reminder to himself "in ye next week to do Master Shakespeare's house in ye Clink Street"! At another time he drew an imaginary portrait of Ben Jonson, supposed to be "copied from a wall portrait in Master Shakespeare's house."

Not content with selling the Captain's originals, Thompson launched a scheme for selling etched reproductions of them and produced a prospectus with a list of subscribers headed by the Prince Consort! Even today "Captain Eyres" are still submitted to the British Museum's Print Room as genuine.

Apart from the deliberate fakes, there are in the exhibition a large number of copies which, though made in the first place without the object of deception, were accepted as originals at some time or other. Ruskin's admiration for Turner resulted in his encouraging many good artists to make copies of the master's water colors, to the confusion of collectors.

Looking at some of these copies hung beside the Turner originals, we get some small idea of the problem with which the experts are faced when one master copies another even greater contemporary. As, for instance, when Andrea del Sarto copied Raphael, or Rembrandt's pupils copied him.

Recalled in a collection of fascinating newspaper cuttings and photographs is the case of the "Leonardo" bust of Flora which nearly caused an international art incident between Germany and Britain before World War I. Though it has been shown conclusively to most experts that the wax bust is a nineteenth-century work, it is still in Berlin's Kaiser Friedrich Museum.

It was bought by the Museum's director, Wilhelm von Bode, in 1909, for £8,000, but no sooner was it put on show than its authenticity was challenged, first by an English art dealer and then by an artist who gloried in the name of Albert Dürer Lucas and who remembered helping his father to make the bust in 1846. It was made in imitation of Leonardo da Vinci but not as a forgery.

Despite the evidence to the contrary von Bode maintained until his death twenty-five years later that he had bought a genuine Leonardo. By trying to save his face in this way he contributed to the popular idea that all art experts are idiots. But though this exhibition recalls many cases where experts have been taken in, it shows far more in which the forger's skill and cunning has been outmatched by the expert's knowledge.

Looking back on it, I see that I adopted a reprehensible attitude to what Mr. John Berger has described* as "one of those crimes for which the cat should be brought back." The too frequent use of the word "fascinating" betrays an attitude toward the forger that makes him out to be a bit of a hero. It is the attitude of the general public, who for some reason, or no reason at all, delight in seeing experts on any subject "taken down a peg or two." The idea has been encouraged by the authors of popular books on the subject who never tire of telling how this or that artist turned to forgery to "get his own back" on the critics who failed to recognize the merits of his genuine pictures. This sort of defense has been claimed for van Meegeren, Jean-Pierre Schecroun (of whom more later) and many others. (The defense of Thompson on the grounds that he was getting his own back on "the government" was even better, since everyone wants to get his own back on "the government"). In some cases it may be true. It is certainly true that many successful forgers have given themselves away because they could not resist the temptation to boast that they had bested the experts. However, it should not be for-

---

* In the *Observer*, July 8, 1962.

gotten that the great majority of forgers do not come into this category, they don't want glory, they are content with money.

How much forgery of works of art is going on today? It is, of course, impossible to say, but it seems certain that more art frauds have been perpetrated during the decade 1955–65 than in any other decade. The faker is as much a part of the art game as the dealer or the restorer or the expert is, and his turnover, like theirs, is in direct proportion to the total amount of art business going on at any particular time. If their business is booming we may take it that his is, too.

Although in 1965 a major art-faking industry was uncovered in Milan, Paris is still undoubtedly the "university city" for forgers. By the mid-1950s the problem there had become so great that a special branch of the Sûreté was set up to deal with it. The mass production of fake late Utrillos after that artist's death in 1955 has provided the police, the artist's widow, and his dealer, M. Paul Pétridès, with a constant headache, and no one with any sense will buy a post–World War I Utrillo nowadays without an unimpeachable provenance to go with it. As any tourist in Paris who has ever seen a Utrillo must know, imitators of the artist's inferior, later works abound there. At least one of these imitators, Madame Claude Latour, was good enough to fool Utrillo himself, although she did not try to. She boasted that she could copy the style of almost any modern artist, but she always signed her pictures with her own name. This, however, was no deterrent to a young dealer with get-rich-quick ideas. He bought her "Utrillos" for a few hundred francs, changed the signature on them and sold them as genuine Utrillos. At the dealer's trial in 1948 Utrillo confessed that he could not be sure that he had not produced some of the Latours exhibited in court. During the following decade Utrillo forgeries were virtually mass-produced. M. Pétridès, who in 1959 published a *catalogue raisonné* of Utrillo's complete *œuvre,* has also recorded over a thousand forgeries that have been brought to his notice.

Recently I was at the home, near Manchester, of that marvelous North Country artist Laurence Stephen Lowry, R.A. (whose work, incidentally, has many affinities with that of Utrillo, although his abstemious and ascetic way of living could not be less like the Frenchman's), when an acquaintance of his called with a "Lowry" he had just bought for a hundred pounds. One glance at it showed it to be a fake. Although the style of the painting bore a super-ficial resemblance to Lowry's style, the picture was signed simply with an *L.* This was obviously done deliberately by the faker—who must have known that Lowry has always signed his work "L. S. Lowry" or occasionally, and early in his career, "L.S.L."—as a "let-out" to cover himself against accusations of forgery. The proud new owner of this thing had called to ask Lowry when he had painted it. As gently as possible he was told that he had been cheated, but, like most people in such circumstances, he was very reluctant to believe this and to Lowry's astonishment he asked, "Are you sure it isn't yours? Isn't there some expert I could take it to for an opinion?" I never saw Lowry angry before or since, but the idea that some "expert" could know more about his own work than he could seemed preposterous. Afterward, when I reminded him that many artists, including Picasso, Augustus John and, above all, Utrillo, had signed works by other men, sincerely believing them to be their own, he laughed and felt sorry for the victim. "Still, it was a bit silly of him to think anyone would give him a picture of mine that size for a hundred pounds nowadays, wasn't it?" said Lowry. And of course he was right.

Unless the sum of money involved is trivial the irresistible bar-gain should always be resisted until one is sure of its authenticity. It is not always easy to resist. In my own case I had to burn my fingers slightly once or twice and then just miss burning them badly before developing resistance. The near-miss also happened in the north. Driving through a small, rather dreary Straffordshire town, I noticed a smart antique shop that seemed out of place. I could see immediately that its stock of furniture was first-class, but what had caught my eye was a little painting that, even at a distance of thirty feet, radiated quality. In the shop I began by examining the furniture, before coming round to the picture as if seeing it for the first time. (Don't ask me why I did this, but, as any dealer will tell you, any customer who thinks he is on to a good find adopts this circuitous sort of approach although it fools nobody.) A brass label on the frame said "Goyen." The subject was fairly typical of Jan van Goyen (1596–1656), a Dutch landscape with the horizon very low down, a few figures on a hillock in the foreground, water in the distance. The color, almost monochrome yellow-brown (the blue in van Goyen's green apparently faded more than two hundred years ago), was made warm where the grain of the panel on which it was painted showed through the pigment. It seemed "right."

"It *is* right," said the dealer.

"Is it signed?" I asked.

"It's signed all over," he said, meaning that the style was unmistakably "right." I examined the picture more closely and was excited to see van Goyen's monogrammed initials, very small, in one corner. Presumably the dealer had missed them. I said nothing, but I was thinking very fast. If the dealer thought it was a genuine van Goyen, as I was beginning to be convinced it was, then the price would be right out of my reach. On the other hand, if the price was the sort that I could afford, then it must be because he knew it was not authentic. Or—but this was unlikely—that he had no idea of the value of a van Goyen.

"How much is it?" I asked.

"Four hundred pounds."

It was a crazy price. As a genuine van Goyen the little picture was worth about £3,000. As a good copy or "school" picture it was worth perhaps £100. I was still no nearer knowing what the dealer really thought, but I was beginning to think if it turned out to be "right" then it was a gift even at £400.

Thinking aloud, I said; "Four hundred?"

"Well, one sold in London last week for seven thousand," he replied.

So he did know. I ought to have asked why he was prepared to let his picture (which was about half the size of the 7,000-guinea one that I had in fact seen sold at Christie's) go for so little. Instead I said, "I'll talk it over with my wife and come back and let you know." And I did talk it over, but I didn't go back. My wife, being a woman and having, therefore, more common sense than any man, decided that we should drive on and forget the nice gentleman who wanted to give us a £3,000 picture for £400 that we hadn't got. We drove on.

For weeks I went on thinking about that picture and wondering if I should have taken a gamble on it. Then one day I saw it again. In a London sale room. It did not look quite so good that time, probably because it was surrounded by some high-class opposition. In the catalogue of the sale it was listed as "van Goyen"— that is, without the "Jan." I asked one of the auctioneers' staff what it was expected to fetch (this, incidentally, is a service any auctioneer will give). To my great relief he said, "Two or three hundred pounds, perhaps." Three days later, when the sale was held, I was there to see the finale of the episode. Bidding for the "van Goyen" began at £50, then rose quickly to £180, at which figure the picture was knocked down in a name I did not recognize. None of the well-known dealers who specialize in Dutch masters had bid. Afterward I asked one of them why he had let it go so cheaply. "Because van Goyen never painted that subject, he only etched it. By the look of the panel it was done from the etching about a hundred years after his death. It was very like his work, but I don't suppose it was ever intended as a forgery.

The signature? That was probably put on about fifty years ago when van Goyen prices began to shoot up."

Offering their wares too cheaply is the commonest mistake made by forgers and fakers and those who try to pass on their productions. This was, I believe, the initial error of judgment that led to the exposure, by London dealer Jacques O'Hana, of the young French forger Jean-Pierre Schecroun. Before one of his accomplices called at the O'Hana Gallery in 1962, Schecroun had succeeded in getting away, to the tune of £25,000, with the forgery of about eighty drawings, water colors and gouaches purporting to be by Picasso and other modern masters. When Mr. O'Hana was offered some of these things he asked for a certificate of authenticity and was given one which was, of course, itself a fake. Schecroun, a skillful artist who had once been a pupil of Fernand Léger, was so well versed in the styles of the artists he faked that he could, for example, produce a wholly convincing brush-and-ink bullfight drawing "by Picasso" in three minutes. Obviously the popular image of the art forger laboring for months to imitate the work of an Old Master is out of date. The breed, of which van Meegeren was king, became redundant with the art boom of the fifties. But it is not only because many modern artists' works now sell for prices comparable with those of Old Masters that forgers now concentrate on producing fake Impressionist and modern pictures. Nor is it because such pictures are "easier to do." It is simply that the forger knows (probably, ironically, as a result of reading about methods of detecting forgeries) that it is always safer for an artist—and don't forget that he is an artist of sorts— to copy or imitate the work of his contemporaries. It is impossible for one artist to adopt the mentality and the spirit of another who lived in a totally different age, and inevitably something of his own time must enter into the fake.

Salvador Dali made this point succinctly when he said that "being a modern painter is the only thing, no matter what you do, that you cannot avoid being." Sepp Schüller, in his book *Forgers, Dealers, Experts* makes it more explicitly:

The counterfeiter is a child of his time, which dictates his outlook. When he attempts to create beauty he falls a victim to the prejudices of his day. He sees and depicts ancient art through the spectacles of his own period. He does not reproduce the work of the old masters but his conception of it as a child of his time. This fact suggests a key to the puzzle of his success as a forger. There is always something "modern" about his productions, which is overlooked by his contemporaries but clearly perceived by a later generation.

It is easy to be wise after the event, but I remember that when I saw some of the van Meegeren forgeries in Amsterdam I was not only amazed that any expert could have been fooled by the terribly poor drawing and shoddy painting of the later "Vermeers" (he became very careless with success) but also struck by the stilted "modernity" of so many of his figures. We may suppose, therefore, that even if the van Meegeren affair had not been blown wide open by the revelation that he had traded with the enemy during World War II (Hermann Goering had acquired by barter one of the "Vermeers" priced at 1,650,000 gulden—£150,-000 then, more than £500,000 today) connoisseurs would one day have discredited them, for even in these days of scientific aids no one has yet improved upon the connoisseur's nose for style as a primary detector of forgery.

Forgeries made in imitation of an artist of several centuries earlier are not, then, the greatest problem for the expert. The deliberate forgery, even that by one artist of another of his own time, is only a minor part of the expert's headache. The great bulk of his work, almost his whole *raison d'être*, is provided by those artists who, without any intention to defraud, copied, imitated or followed the style of masters of their own time whom they admired or of whom they were pupils.

Often the problem is so great that the authorship of a great masterpiece becomes a question of, as *The New Yorker* would put it, "which expert d'ya follow?" S. N. Behrman* tells how the great dealer Joseph Duveen tried to sell to Andrew Mellon a painting which he and many experts believed to be by Giorgione. Mellon was delighted with the picture but wanted to know what the "infallible" Bernard Berenson's attribution would be. "There isn't a doubt in the world that B.B. will say it's a Giorgione," Duveen assured him. But he was wrong. Berenson decided it was an early Titian, "perhaps his earliest work, but only half out of the egg, the other half still in the Giorgione formula." Mellon refused the picture. Duveen, bloody-minded but by no means bowed, found another millionaire to buy it and, to avenge himself, contrived that it should ultimately go to the National Gallery, Washington, which was given to the American people by Mellon and houses his collection. The picture, *The Adoration of the Shepherds,* is there now. It is attributed to Giorgione.

The picture is, of course, the same picture whether it is ascribed to Giorgione or to Titian. Why, then, you may ask, does it matter so much who painted it? Especially in this case where both artists are great masters? The answer is for the most part that old thing— money. There is among scholars, of course, a disinterested desire to get at the truth in such cases, but what could it have mattered to Mellon? True, he already owned plenty of Titians, but the *Adoration* was unlike anything he had and he professed to be enraptured by it. However, although he had to rely upon experts to do his aesthetics for him he could do his own mathematics, and he knew that if the painting was by Titian then Duveen was asking several hundred thousand dollars too much. For Titian, the pupil of Giorgione, has not his master's virtue of great rarity. He lived to be ninety-nine and never stopped working. Giorgione

---

* *Op. cit.*

died at thirty-three and the number of pictures that can be attributed to him with certainty is less than a dozen.

Now let us imagine that Berenson had pronounced the picture to be, not by Titian, but by Palma Vecchio (this did, in fact, happen to another "Giorgione" when Philip Hendy, the present director of the National Gallery, London, prepared a catalogue of another American millionaire's collection), who was influenced by Giorgione and was, like him, a pupil of Giovanni Bellini. This would have knocked another hundred thousand dollars off Mellon's estimate of the picture's value. Yet it would have been the same picture. And it would have been the same picture if finally the great B.B., who once said, "Never stick to a mistake," had announced that he had decided it was by none of these but was a copy of a lost Giorgione by an unknown sixteenth- or seventeenth-century artist. Then the picture would have been comparatively valueless. But it would still have been the same picture.

This may sound farfetched, but similar, if not quite such spectacular, things are happening all the time. In 1954 the London dealer Leonard Koetser paid 6,000 guineas at Christie's for what most dealers must have thought was a copy of a *Madonna* by the Bolognese master Francesco Francia (*c.* 1450–1517), the original of which was in the National Gallery. But Koetser claimed that his picture was the original and the Gallery picture the copy. Under pressure from Koetser and others the Gallery's scientists went to work and had to admit that he was right. The picture (which, incidentally, had been "declared genuine" by the near-infallible Bernard Berenson) proved to be a skillfully executed, but now worthless, nineteenth-century forgery.

Few weeks pass without a report of some "exposure" making headlines in the press somewhere. In 1961 a Munich art dealer, Mr. Martin Porkay, declared that a newly acquired Rembrandt in the Kunsthalle at Bremen was not by Rembrandt. Newspaper reports of the affair claimed for Mr. Porkay that in 1937 he had shown that a £130,000 Masaccio *Madonna* in Washington's National Gallery was by a twentieth-century Viennese artist, and that among his other "successes" were the discovery of a fake van Eyck and a fake Rembrandt in Budapest and the detection of two fake Rembrandts in the Alte Pinakothek in Munich.

In 1962 the press stirred up what the *Sunday Express* described as "one of the stormiest controversies in the art world for years" over twin versions of Rubens' *Diana and Her Nymphs,* one of which belongs to Mr. Paul Getty, who was said to have paid £200,000 for it shortly before. The second version had been bought by the Cleveland Museum of Art for "more than £100,-000" in 1958. The question was, "Which twin has the master touch?" Said the *Sunday Express:*

Only one painting can be the original. The other is likely to be a studio copy with finishing touches added by the master, and worth only a small fraction of its price.

Other famous artists frequently made several copies of their works. Could Rubens have painted both pictures? Unlikely, for although he often did several versions of the same subject the paintings are much too meticulously similar for both to be from his brush.

The painting which is finally acclaimed as the original deserves to rank in importance beside Rubens's *Adoration of the Magi,* which fetched £275,000 at a London auction in 1959.

What an extraordinary statement that last paragraph is, but how well it crystallizes the crazy illogic of the art game, a house of cards built on the often infirm shoulders of the experts. Here are two very fine paintings, each believed by different experts to be by that busy mass-producer-of-pictures and diplomat Sir Peter Paul Rubens. While they are in dispute each is worth a fortune. But if and when the dispute is resolved in favor of the one, the other will be comparatively worthless. Yet they will still, like Duveen's "Giorgione," be the same pictures.

In the case of Rubens, more than that of any other artist, such a situation is ridiculous because in nearly all his large canvases he employed assistants. Some of them, like Van Dyck, who was his pupil, and Frans Snyders, who was his studio manager, were masters in their own right, and it is impossible to say with any certainty how much of them is by *the* master. According to one American art historian Rubens was as bogus as Baconians believe Shakespeare to have been. Rubens, more businessman than artist according to this theory, continuously passed off the work of others, especially Snyders, as his own. Farfetched as such a theory may be, it is not entirely without basis in the light of the way in which Rubens' studio operated, nor in the light of his own statements. Until the eighteenth century the artist was regarded as a craftsman like any other craftsman, who, when the demand for his work became too much for him, employed assistants to help him. Only the crankiest or most fastidious of patrons commissioning a successful painter would have thought of insisting that the master must carry out the entire commission himself. So, in 1618, we find Rubens replying to Sir Dudley Carlton, who wanted to acquire some of his paintings but insisted that they be all his own work, that certain pictures were not copies, "because they have been retouched so skilfully by my own hand that they can hardly be distinguished from the originals." And of a particular picture he wrote, "As this reproduction is not yet finished I am going to retouch it throughout myself. So it will pass for an original if necessary." After Sir Dudley had rejected such things Rubens offered him other pictures which, he said, were entirely his work except that *as was his custom* he had had the landscape backgrounds painted by a man who was very good at that particular job.

The chances of either the Getty picture or the Cleveland picture being *entirely* by Rubens would seem, then, to be very slender, but by examining them side by side experts could probably add considerably to their knowledge and perhaps agree on the extent to which the master's hand is evident in each. When so much money is at stake, however, owners of paintings are often understandably reluctant to get at the truth. But in fairness to Mr. Getty it should be recalled that when, in 1964, he was told that a painting he bought for £40 at Sotheby's in 1938 was probably a genuine Raphael worth £250,000 or more, he remarked, "I really don't mind whether it is the original Raphael or not. I just know I like it." Fortunately for the art game, only the very rich can afford to take this attitude. It would never do for everyone to go around buying what he likes instead of what the experts and dealers tell him he ought to like.

(Since writing the above I have heard that Mr. Getty was later seen studying art books in the British Museum Library in an attempt to authenticate his picture.* This is good news. There is more rejoicing in the art game over the one who was lost and is found than over the ninety and nine who were never lost. Especially when the one is a multimillionaire.)

For anyone contemplating joining the fakes-and-forgeries department of the game it may be of interest to note that among the reasons given by experts for believing that Mr. Getty's Rubens and Raphael are original works by these masters is the fact that each has been shown, by X-ray or infrared radiation, to have undergone changes in design during the painting process. These *pentimenti,* as they are called, may suggest to the forger a way of giving to his work an added semblance of authenticity, but he must remember that if he does so he must also find a way of making them appear like the real thing when his pictures are submitted to X-ray, infrared or ultraviolet radiation techniques. Ironically, the best guides to the forger's art were, for a long time, those books

---

* In June 1966 the Metropolitan Museum decided that the picture *is* Raphael's *Madonna di Loreto*—valued at over $1,000,000.

devoted to methods of investigating paintings and uncovering fakes. Today science has outstripped the forger of Old Master paintings. The Milliprobe, invented by Dr. Edward Hall and recently put to use at the National Gallery in London, can analyze the chemical elements in a painting and print the results on an electric typewriter in a matter of minutes. Thus elaborate forgeries are now hardly worth the candle, and it may well be that van Meegeren was the last of his kind.

Obviously chemical analysis cannot play so important a part in the detection of forgeries purporting to be works painted during the past hundred years or so, when the use of mass-produced pigments became more or less universal. This is yet another very good reason why nearly all the forgeries we encounter nowadays are of Impressionist or later pictures. From my own observations I have come to the conclusion that even in this field the forger's outlook has changed radically in the last few years. Looking at the art market as it is today, he has evidently decided that lots of quick small profits are as good as, if not better than, a few slow big ones. Instead of concentrating on the big killing that will bring in a few thousand pounds, he aims to catch scores of little fish. The great advantage of this is that there is virtually no risk involved.

In Chapter Five, you will remember, I referred to the trick of buying up quantities of old water colors by unidentified artists, usually of the nineteenth century, attaching to them (either by way of a false signature or simply by lettering on a mount) the name of some famous artist, and putting them into any sale room that will take them (and all too many will). In recent years the trick has been brought more up to date, and the names or initials of modern masters are associated with drawings and paintings that often have little resemblance to the works of those masters. The trap is intended to catch the large numbers of novice collectors who now buy direct from the sale rooms and are always hoping to make, and thinking they have made, a find. It may be a petty kind of fraud, but it is a particularly cunning one, for in the unlikely event of a victim trying to get redress he will almost certainly find he has no legal leg to stand on. He has only his own stupidity to blame. Here are a few examples, seen recently in minor London sale rooms, of the sort of thing I have in mind:

1. A nude drawing, signed with an *M* in a circle.
2. Another nude, signed "John."
3. A head of a woman, signed "HM."
4. A water color of a French lawyer, signed "hD."

In each case the signature was a good imitation of that of a famous artist—the *M* for Maillol, "John" for Augustus John, "HM" for Matisse and "hD" for Daumier—but the drawings, although competent, bore no particular resemblance to the work of these artists. Nevertheless they were deliberately intended to deceive someone into thinking that they might perhaps be early works, or works of an unfamiliar period, by those artists.

But let us suppose that you or I have bought these drawings for an average of, say, twenty pounds each and then we find that none of them is what we thought or hoped. We complain to the auctioneers. They draw our attention to the clause in their conditions of sale that says they are not responsible for errors of description, etc., and, in any case, they never said these drawings were by any of the artists we named (they were catalogued as nineteenth- or twentieth-century French or English schools, or some such). We ask who put them into the sale and are told that is a confidence they cannot possibly break without the seller's permission. Let us imagine, however, that we do track down the vendor (he is probably a small-time dealer) and put our questions to him. He looks at us pityingly and says, "If I thought they were by the people you say, do you think I would be daft enough to put them into that sale? As far as I know the *M* is for Morris, 'John' is for John Smith, 'HM' is Harry Mudd and 'hD' is for hot dog." And as a parting shot he adds, "If you know anywhere where you can buy a Matisse or a Daumier for twenty pounds let me know!" And of course he is right, we have been fools. But we have learned a lesson and we will write the lost money off to "experience," while the confidence trickster—that is, I suppose, what he is—goes on finding new victims.

The only people who could do anything about this sort of thing are those auctioneers who are being used as distributing agents, wittingly in most cases. But usually their attitude is that if people are fools they must take the consequences. After all, they say, the buyer himself is hoping to get something for nothing or, at least, for far below its real price. Because they themselves are too experienced to be caught by such elementary tricks, members of the art trade take these petty frauds far too lightly even when they are perpetrated by some of their own less reputable colleagues. I remember being shocked a few years ago when, after watching an unsigned picture catalogued as nineteenth-century French school knocked down in a London sale room for an unexpectedly good price, a member of the auctioneer's picture staff remarked with a laugh, "I bet that has a signature on it next time I see it." It certainly had next time I saw it—in a dealer's gallery a few hundred yards from the sale room!

In this case the dealer would probably have argued that the painting was undoubtedly by the artist whose name it bore and that he would never attach a signature to any picture unless he was sure it was the right one. He would probably have argued, too, that his clients insisted on signed works and that it was, therefore, their fault if he had to do a little bit of jiggery-pokery to please them. There are collectors who, without any ability to recognize any particular artist's work, foolishly put far too much faith in a signature. Even the artist's name written on a drawing,

The poor quality of Picasso paintings available to the collector with less than £20,000 to spend is shown in the first two illustrations here. *La Commode Chinoise*, above left, 58 in. x 45 in., cost £17,000 at Sotheby's in November 1964. *Le Vieux Musicien*, above right, 20¾ in. x 25 in., cost £5,500 at Christie's in the same month. Even with £50,000 the collector will have a hard time finding a Picasso of any importance. The trivial but large (63¾ in. x 51 in.) *Femme assise sur une Chaise*, right, was bought for that sum by Wildenstein, the dealers, at Sotheby's in June 1965.

Van Gogh's *Les Déchargeurs* was bought by Marlborough Fine Art at Sotheby's in 1959 for £30,000. In June 1963 it reappeared at Sotheby's as the property of the wealthy collector Mrs. Derek Fitzgerald but failed to reach whatever reserve price had been put on it and was bought in at £45,000. Two years later Sotheby's, who were now in control of Parke-Bernet, the New York auctioneers who had been their rivals, sent the picture across the Atlantic to be sold. It came up at Parke-Bernet's in April 1965—and was sold for $240,000 (£85,700).

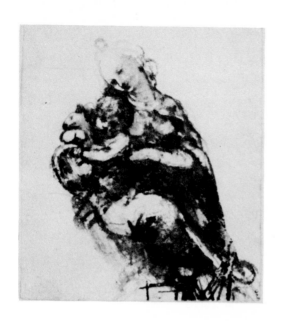

These two drawings are reproduced actual size. *Madonna and Child with a Cat*, above, by Leonardo da Vinci, is 3¼ in. x 2¾ in. *Ascanius Pulling Aeneas Away from Dido's Bed*, right, by Michelangelo, is 3¾ in. x 2⅞ in. The Leonardo was sold at Sotheby's in 1963 for £19,000—more than £2,100 a square inch. The Michelangelo fetched £12,500 in the same sale room in 1964. The Leonardo is a charming little sketch but nothing more. Its price would buy a superb and important drawing by almost any other master except Michelangelo and Raphael. Only in the mad world of stamp collecting will you find crazier prices than this.

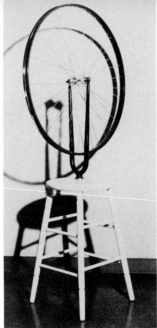

The construction called *Bicycle Wheel,* above left, was made by Marcel Duchamp in 1913. It was the earliest of his "assisted ready-mades," mass-produced articles which, it was (and still is) claimed, have been transformed into works of art by "a little inspired alteration." It has been described as "the first major incidence of wholly non-art elements paradoxically challenging the esthetic frame of reference." The other three pictures show: above right, *Untitled American President,* 1962, a mixed-media construction by Edward Kienholz; left top, *Big Baked Potato,* 1963, a painted sculpture of plaster, cloth and sponge, by Claes Oldenburg; and an untitled, mixed-media sculpture of 1959, left bottom, by Lee Bontecou. Kienholz, Oldenburg and Bontecou are but three of the hundreds of contemporary American artists of whom it has been said that 78-year-old Duchamp is their patron saint. But ideas that were startling and revolutionary in 1913 are bound to have worn a bit thin fifty years later, however much they may be disguised and dressed up—or even blown up, as when Oldenburg made an 11-foot-long ice-cream cone and his notorious 7 ft. x 4 ft. hamburger.

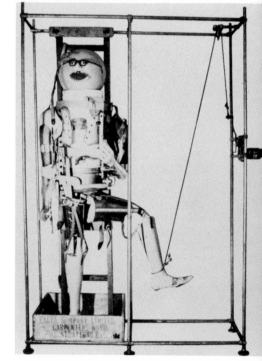

Tom Wesselman's *Bathtub Collage 3* is one of a long series of works in which this American so-called New Realist artist combines painted nudes with elements of real furniture, fixtures and fittings. Here, the curtain, the bathmat, laundry basket, door, towel, electric-light switch, etc., are all real. In later creations he introduced such refinements as the taped sound of street noises and "real" pubic hair made of fur. Bruce Lacey's *Boy, Oh Boy, am I living!*, 1964, is a "rubbish construction" made from artificial limbs, a water-heater, balloon, other "found objects" and a somewhat sardonic English sense of humor. An electric motor keeps the figure's left leg kicking gaily. Lacey, who is an actor as well as an artist, has an uncanny talent for injecting a sense of pathos and an element of social comment into such works as this.

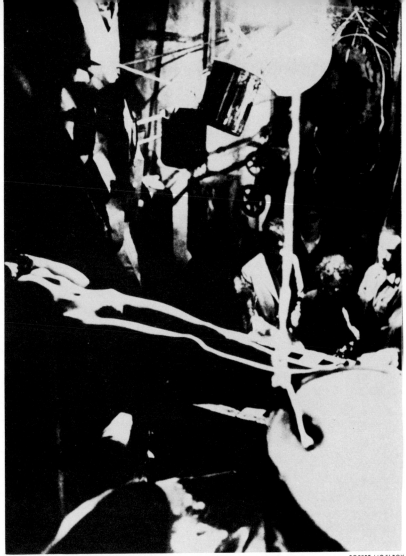

The scene in the boiler room of New York's Maidman Playhouse, during a "happening"—later titled *A Service for the Dead*—created by American artist Allan Kaprow with the aid of a nude model (the "corpse"), a group of bum musicians, garbage cans, paint buckets, dirty water, bad smells, oil fumes and a number of invited participants. This elaborate and sophisticated type of "happening" is largely an American product evolved by artists like Kaprow and Claes Oldenburg from "pictures" which were becoming more and more three-dimensional, pushing out into space and enveloping the spectator. It is far removed from the sort of "happening" that was created in the street in France and involved unsuspecting passersby in an "experience" wholly unanticipated. Behind the Happenings Movement is the idea that the barrier between artist and public must be destroyed and that the artist's role is no longer to create objects that may arouse sensations in others but to arouse sensations by direct action in which the public participates.

BRAM WISMAN

These two views of a world of the future—the new Babylon—are taken from models made by the Dutch artist Constant (Constant Nieuwenhuys), who in a speech delivered at the Institute of Contemporary Arts, London, in November 1963, said: "Since all the work will be done by machines the new man will be free to spend his life, like a nomad, traveling through the ever-changing New Babylon and sampling some of the intense and gratifying experiences it will provide. The energies now devoted to work will be spent on the development of man's creative capacities in the worldwide city, which will be a sort of enormous playground. It will consist basically of flexible living sectors with open spaces in between for parks, agricultural lands and gardens, covering the entire surface of the earth. The environment will alter according to the desires and activities of the passing Homo ludens. In this flux of change and movement the common creative force will create a collective mood and atmosphere (something like collective poetry) which will be both the aim and the justification of the life of this new nomadic race."

The author (right) at work taking notes, as American collector Norton Simon, finger raised reprovingly, protests to the auctioneer during the sensational sale at Christie's on March 19, 1965. Immediately before this photograph was taken Rembrandt's *Titus* had been knocked down to Marlborough Fine Art at 740,-000 guineas. But after Mr. Simon had objected that he was still bidding, the picture was put up again and sold to him at 760,000 guineas. The incident spotlighted an aspect of sale-room procedure of which the general public knew nothing—the business of "secret bids" and "bidding codes."

without any attempt at forging his signature, will satisfy many buyers, especially if the drawing is old and the name is written in an old-fashioned hand. I know one collector of drawings who will have nothing but signed works, and so his collection includes several "signed" drawings by artists who are known never to have signed their work. The fact that a spurious signature will throw suspicion on a genuine drawing does not seem to have occurred to him. So long as such collectors exist there will be unscrupulous dealers who will satisfy their demands. A signature is superfluous to an unimpeachable drawing and it can add nothing to a drawing that is not "right." The aim of the collector must be to learn to recognize artists' styles, not just their signatures.

In his biography of Lucien Pissarro, W. S. Meadmore tells a classic story about signature-faking and shows, at the same time, how inadequate the law is to counter it. In the years just before the last war Lucien Pissarro, artist son of the great Impressionist master Camille Pissarro, was preparing the complete catalogue of his father's works, when a friend reported that he had seen a Camille Pissarro in a small-time dealer's shop window. Lucien went to see the picture and recognized it as one of his own landscapes, which had been sold at Sotheby's in December 1936 for £22. But now his own signature had been removed and replaced with an imitation of his father's "C. Pissarro." After establishing that the shopkeeper was in fact the man who had bought the picture at Sotheby's he took legal advice and was told, to his dismay, that "forgery of this description was not considered a criminal action under English law." He could try taking an action for damages, but it would be difficult, said his solicitors, to convince a court that having one of his paintings passed off as the work of a great master had been damaging to his reputation!

Lucien persisted and made an application at Bow Street for a prosecution on the grounds of false pretenses, but by this time the picture had been sold (for £450) to a buyer who could not be traced, and the magistrate ruled that unless the picture could be produced no case could be brought. Still Lucien fought on, and eventually the case came up at the Old Bailey but was again dismissed. "Now there is, of course, no doubt," Lucien Pissarro wrote afterward, "that the case was tried perfectly fairly, and that the result was in accordance with the law. May one not suspect, however, that if a grocer had offered for sale margarine as fresh butter the result would have been different?"

One law for grocers and another for art dealers? The dealer in this case certainly seems to have made his own law. His shop was filled with fakes to which he added appropriate signatures. If a customer brought a picture back he said that he had sold it in good faith and immediately gave the customer his money back.

I was particularly interested to read in Mr. Meadmore's account that some of these fakes were produced by an artist in Manchester at thirty shillings each. In 1964 when I went to Manchester to visit a number of private collectors I heard repeatedly of a dealer, in business there until he died some years ago, who could always satisfy collectors' requirements with suspicious promptitude. No matter what a customer yearned for, the dealer always knew where he could get hold of one. A Constable? A Sickert? A Manet? Someone he knew had the very thing. It would take only a few days to get it. From what I saw it appeared that the dealer kept a sizable stock of fairly good-quality paintings and drawings by unknown artists, and from this he chose one that had some (often very slight) stylistic resemblance to the work of the master his client admired. All he needed then was a few days' drying time for the signature he would add to the picture (drawings did not take so long to procure!).

Before we leave this business of the signature racket a special word of warning about its application to prints—lithographs, etchings, woodcuts, etc.—may be of some help. It is one which I can give with the conviction that comes from a chastening personal experience in which I was saved, by the superior knowledge of the dealers at an auction sale, from paying far too much for a Picasso lithograph. Modern prints, as the reader will know, are usually issued in limited editions in which each work is numbered and signed by the artist. But there are also unlimited editions, made by artists popular enough to be able to command a mass market, that are signed only "in the stone"—that is to say the artist puts his signature on the lithographic stone or plate so that it is reproduced with the drawing. The art market being what it is, the limited-edition print is invariably far more valuable than the unlimited-edition print, which is usually printed by an automatic process and not by hand. The difference, however, will be obvious only to those who have some knowledge of this very tricky field, and, once again, the addition of a penciled signature and, for extra verisimilitude, a few numerals will be enough to fool the rest of us.

It was, at any rate, enough to fool me on that day when I bid in a London sale room for a lithograph described in the catalogue as "signed in the stone." I had noticed at the preview that, in spite of the description, the print also bore Picasso's signature and the numbers "27/75" (meaning that it was number twenty-seven in an edition of seventy-five). Thinking that the catalogue compiler had missed these details, I hoped to get it cheaply, and I was very happy when it was knocked down to me for £12. It was only later that I realized I must have been the only person in the sale room who did not know that it was from an unlimited edition and that the pencil signature was a fake. Had there been another ignoramus in the room he or I might have been forced to pay much more for it. As it was, I paid about the same price as that for which I could have bought it in any printseller's shop.

There are so many of these spurious prints around that it is always advisable for the nonexpert to buy only from established art dealers or printsellers. Recently the wife of a well-known painter told me how, while traveling on the Continent, she found a print stall in a street market and decided to make her husband a present of a signed etching by an artist he greatly admired. She asked the price—£25—and then went to get her husband to see it before she paid up. But the street trader recognized the painter immediately, quickly put the etching out of sight and said, "Sorry, sir, but it's not for you." His stock, he said, all came from his private collection, which he was reluctantly obliged to sell. Enquiries showed that he had been selling the "collection" for many years.

It is not my purpose to repeat here the hundreds of intriguing accounts of forgers' and fakers' methods that have made so many very readable books. All I have tried to do is to indicate to the novice collector how much there is to learn and how important it is to be extremely cautious in the early stages. What I hope I have not done is to create such a frightening impression of an art market bedeviled with forgeries and fakes that the beginner will be scared off. If he goes about the business of collecting intelligently he need have no great fear of serious losses, and such losses as he may suffer need be no more than he is prepared to pay for experience and for the thrill of the game. Out-and-out forgeries, that is to say works deliberately made in imitation of other works for fraudulent ends, are unlikely to concern him at all until he is ready to spend considerable sums of money, and by that time he should be experienced enough not to be an easy victim. In any case, forgeries are less common than the publicity given to them probably suggests. One should be wary of those gentlemen who seek to establish themselves as experts by wholesale denunciations of "forgeries," one of whom wrote to me when the Thyssen collection was exhibited at the National Gallery in 1961 claiming that only eighteen out of 118 pictures on show were genuine! Fakes—that is, pictures to which alterations or additions have been made in order that they may be passed off as more valuable works, and copies made, originally at least, without any intention of fraud—will, however, be encountered again and again. Without them the art game would be as dull as cricket. The one way to avoid them is to be well-off enough and dull enough always to buy only through established dealers. And even that, as we have seen in the case of Mr. Getty, does not guarantee absolute freedom from excitement and controversy.

So far in this chapter I have discussed only ways in which you may be cheated or may cheat yourself when you are buying a picture. But you may also be cheated when you are selling a picture. And even while you are sitting at home without the slightest thought of selling a picture it is possible that there is a "knocker" not far away plotting to separate you from your family heirloom for a little of its true value. In Britain (and no doubt in other countries, too) he may one day knock on your door, hand you his card and say, "Good morning, madam" (he rarely calls when husbands are at home), "forgive me for troubling you" (he is very polite), "but I have an urgent order from America for pieces of Victoriana—glass, furniture, pictures and so on. It doesn't matter about the condition as long as it is the right age. We will take almost any old thing you want to get rid of and we pay the best prices. You haven't anything? You would be surprised, madam. If you just let me have a quick look round I can give you an idea of the sort of thing I have in mind. Why, even that old umbrella stand there could be worth ten pounds to you."

This is where you should say, "No, thank you," and shut the door. But ten pounds for that horrible old umbrella stand! Heavens, he might take that terrible old brass fender and fire irons that you haven't used since the central heating was put in. You are sunk, he is inside now and his eyes are whizzing round the place pricing everything like an electronic cash register. Funny thing, he doesn't seem to look at all at the things you thought were rather good. At this stage he may ask to see upstairs (or, if he has brought an accomplice along—they often hunt in pairs—the accomplice may ask where the "loo" is and have a quick snoop round while looking for it). Up there he goes through the same calculating motions. He admires some of your furniture (it's reproduction) but regrets that it is the "wrong period." You show him the brass fender in the junk room and you are just about to beg him to take it away for nothing when he says, "Can't offer you more than five pounds for it. Not much demand for them nowadays." You are delighted. He rummages around the junk while you assure him there is nothing else there. On his way out of the room he notices, apparently for the first time, that old picture in the gilt frame that you threw out of the drawing room when you redecorated last year. "Would you like to sell that frame?" he asks. It's a terrible, dull, heavy Victorian gilt thing, so you say yes. "Just the sort of thing they like in America," he says. "Give you a fiver for that too." He picks it up to take downstairs. "Don't forget the fender," you say and he laughs and picks that up too.

At the front door he takes out his wallet bulging with fivers, of which he hands you two. He has forgotten about the umbrella stand and you don't like to ask him about that, but you say timidly, "I thought you only wanted the frame, not the picture." Maybe he will give you a couple more pounds, you think. Instead he laughs and says, "Oh, I'm sorry. Of course I don't want the picture." And he begins to fumble with the back to get it out of the frame. When he asks you for a hammer and pliers you probably say, "Oh, don't bother," and let him keep the picture. If you bring him the hammer and pliers he will probably say, "Oh, it doesn't matter. I won't take the frame," and put out his hand for you to return one of the fivers. Or he may offer you a few pounds for the picture, which is, he says, "just a print" or "an amateurish copy." He may, of course, be right. Unless your husband comes home and says, "My God! That was the family Turner you've given away!" you will probably never know. Only one thing is certain: the knocker did not pay you more than it was worth. He is going to make a profit, perhaps only 100 per cent, perhaps 100,000 per cent.

This is an old-fashioned technique. Modern knockers have many much cleverer methods, the most diabolical of which was explained to me by a picture expert at a London sale room who had just had a painful interview with a gentleman from the north, who had been cheated out of more than £8,000. The gentleman had answered a newspaper advertisement which said that the guardian of certain trustee funds wished to purchase fine paintings as an investment. On receipt of his letter the "trustee" came to see him and was shown a painting by the famous English equestrian artist Ben Marshall. It looked a very fine picture, but naturally the "trustee" had to be sure of its value. He requested, and was granted, permission to bring it to the London sale room for a valuation. He was given a valuation of several thousand pounds but then went back to the owner and said he had been told that the picture was not authentic. In spite of this he was willing to give the disappointed man two hundred pounds for it. The offer was accepted and the new owner brought the picture straight to London and put it into the sale room, where, a few weeks later, it sold for 8,000 guineas. There the matter would have ended had it not been for the fact that the picture was mentioned in a report of the sale published in the original owner's favorite newspaper.

This was a case of deliberate fraud. Most knockers would not go so far. Like the members of the "rings" (see the next chapter), they argue that their successes are made possible only by the stupidity of the public, but, unlike the ring men, they do not consistently break the law. Generally you will never know what happens to the picture you sell to a knocker for, say, five pounds. But if you learn that he has sold it for a thousand and challenge him, he can always answer that, at the time, he thought he was giving you a fair price. And there is nothing you can do about that.

In view of all the publicity given to the high prices paid for pictures, it is surprising that the knockers can still find any victims. But they do, and often in the most unlikely places. In 1963 Sotheby's were surprised when a man brought to them an extraordinary picture called *The Fairy Feller's Masterstroke*, by the nineteenth-century artist Richard Dadd, who went mad, killed his father and spent the remaining forty-four years of his life in Bethlem and Broadmoor. The only published record of the picture showed that it had been in the collection of Siegfried Sassoon, and this fact was recorded in the catalogue of the sale in which it was to have been sold on May 29, 1963. But at the last moment the picture was withdrawn from the sale without explanation. Then a few weeks later it appeared among a number of new acquisitions on show at the Tate Gallery. With it was a note explaining that it had been presented to the Tate by Siegfried Sassoon. Obviously something very fishy had been going on and no one wanted to talk about it, but my suspicion that a knocker was concerned in the affair was confirmed. Although I have met several knockers, none has ever tried to charm anything out of me. Indeed, I would not wish to meet a less charming bunch of men. Yet the evidence shows that there is one born every minute to whom they are irresistible.

Ever since I heard the story about the Ben Marshall picture I have looked with suspicion at all "agony-column" advertisements about pictures wanted and about pictures for sale too. I have only once replied to one of the latter. It offered "original drawings by modern British artists—Spencer, Sickert, Epstein, John, Paul Nash and Matthew Smith" (all of whom were dead) and gave a Hampstead telephone number. The voice that answered when I rang was very warm and keen until I gave my name. Then it decided that there was not really any point in my making the journey to

Hampstead, because the drawings were only odds and ends. "Not good enough for you, old man," said the voice. And I was cut off without being given any address. Still, it would be foolish to suggest that all advertisements of this kind are traps. There are often good reasons why both genuine buyers and genuine sellers use this method of doing business. All I am advocating is caution. If you are selling, make sure you know what it is you are selling and have some idea of its market value. If you are buying, don't be afraid to ask for assurances of authenticity; a good dealer will guarantee to take a picture back if you prove his description of it to be false. Be particularly careful about advertisements that say, "No dealers." This is tantamount to saying, "No one with any knowledge wanted."

If I have made the whole business of collecting sound terribly hazardous, that is as it should be. But don't be completely discouraged. Elsewhere in this book I hope you will find useful advice on how to go about playing the art game with the maximum of pleasure at a cost you can afford and with the prospect of ultimate profit hanging like a carrot just a little way ahead and growing fatter and juicier the longer you leave it.

7

Ring-a-Ring
o' Rogues

An auction is a publick sale,
That injures those who fairly deal.
—Verse from an
eighteenth-century print

Some years ago I attended a North Country sale of pictures which
turned out to be an almost complete compendium of the booby
traps which may be laid, consciously or unconsciously, for the
unwary. The catalogue listed works by almost every distinguished
water-colorist from Paul Sandby to Wilson Steer, included the
inevitable "Corot" and concluded with a few things by such artists as Munnings and John. It was obviously too good to be true
and it meant a journey of two hundred miles, but once you have
the sale-room bug you don't let little things like those deter you.
I went.

Before the sale began there were two hours for viewing, but it took only a minute to see that it was a very curious sale. About sixty per cent of the property was junk, about thirty-five per cent was the sort of odds and ends that sell for a few pounds in the smaller London sale rooms, and about five per cent was made up of drawings and paintings of some quality. A large proportion of the drawings and water colors had, apparently, been newly mounted and framed for the sale, and a surprisingly large number of the other pictures bore the marks of a London auction room on their backs. From these two facts I drew the conclusions that those things in the first category had been put into the sale by a dealer and that most of those in the second had been considered but not accepted for sale in London. In both cases the signs read "Proceed with caution," for dealers do not usually sell works by "big names" in the country unless they have first tried to get them sold in London, and London sale rooms do not turn down "big names" unless they are, to put it mildly, skeptical of them.

Again there was an unusually high proportion of mounts and frames bearing the names of famous artists—Peter de Wint, Paul Sandby, Francis Towne, John Sell Cotman, Myles Birket Foster, and so on. All were competent and many were charming old water colors and drawings, but the "de Wint" was not a de Wint, the "Sandby" was not a Sandby, the "Towne" was not a Towne, the "Cotman" was not a Cotman, and the "Myles Birket Foster" was not a Myles Birket Foster in spite of its bearing a monogram that looked very like his. And needless to say the two "Corots" were nothing like Corots although they were in frames labeled "J. B. Corot." A drawing signed "John" may have been by John Somebody-or-other, but it was certainly not, as the catalogue claimed, by Augustus John. Yet a good horsy thing by Munnings was unmistakably "right," and, even more unexpected in this sort of company, there was a seventeenth-century Dutch interior of

first-class quality. It was catalogued baldly as "an old picture
of peasants in an inn."

It was this last painting that attracted most attention, and I
noticed many men whom I took to be dealers or dealers' runners
examining it closely. But when the sale began none of these dealers was present. The auctioneer was agonizingly slow. After an
hour he had sold only forty out of the two hundred lots. (At
Sotheby's and Christie's the rate is at least twice as high, and in
some of the other London sale rooms they move three times as
fast.)

I left the room for a breather. In the pub next door six or seven
of the missing dealers were sitting talking. I stood at the bar with
a drink and listened. They were discussing what they could do
about a gentleman named Weston who had refused repeatedly
to join them. I realized that I was in the presence of "the ring."
When I turned to look at them, the man who was evidently their
leader put a finger to his lips and silenced them.

When I returned to the sale room the auctioneer was nearing
Lot 100 but there was still another hour to go before the best
things would be sold. A few minutes before the hour was up the
seven dealers came in and stood near the door. Another few
minutes more and they moved into the body of the room, and one
of them separated from the others and took up a position where
he could be easily seen by the auctioneer—and by his fellow dealers. The Dutch picture came up and the auctioneer asked for
"ten pounds to start." The lone dealer nodded. The price went
fairly quickly to forty pounds and stopped. Instead of coaxing his
audience for more bids as he had done *ad nauseam* throughout
the sale, the auctioneer seemed anxious to knock the picture down
quickly. "All done at forty pounds, then," he said and raised his
hammer. I waved my catalogue at him. I had had no intention
of bidding, because I had estimated that the picture would fetch
at least £250, but now I made up my mind to bid up to one
hundred. I did not expect to get it for that, but the indecent haste

with which the auctioneer wanted to knock it down to the ring needled me into determination that they should pay a reasonable price for it. I went on bidding to a hundred—and beyond. Suddenly, at £110, the ring's man shook his head. "Yours, sir," the auctioneer said, bringing down his hammer with a harder-than-usual bang. "May I have your name please." Unexpectedly I was the owner of "an old picture of peasants in an inn." It turned out to be, as I had at first guessed and later hoped, a work of David Teniers the Younger.

This was my first firsthand experience of a ring at work. On two or three occasions since, I have made very good buys by outbidding rings in smaller sale rooms and in private-house sales, but I doubt whether one would be allowed to make a habit of it without some attempt by them to stop it. I often wondered what they did to poor Mr. Weston. I doubt that they were content simply to damage the things he bought before he took possession of them, which is what they might do to anything for which you or I outbid them.

For a reason that I shall explain later, it is fairly certain that if you outbid a ring for something you really want you will get it at a very reasonable price—unless they happen to be deliberately taking you for a ride. But it is as well to be warned against the idea that if you outbid a reputable dealer you will necessarily do the same. The dealer may be bidding on behalf of a wealthy client who wants the picture at any price. And, of course, both he and you may be making a mistake.

Rings are illegal, but, as in the case I have described, the law is brazenly and continuously flouted in the country sale rooms. In London the members of a ring will work more discreetly, the amount of discretion increasing with the quality of the sale room, and in the top sale rooms their activities are greatly restricted for the simple reason that they can rarely get a look in there. Obviously they must depend for their successes on the ignorance of buyers outside their ring, but in any important sale in London

they come up against the vastly superior knowledge of the big
dealers and, in the case of Sotheby's and Christie's, the knowledge
of the firm's back-room boys, which is made available to everyone
through the catalogue.

Talk of *"the* ring" suggests a single tight organization that
travels from sale to sale in a body. In practice a ring is formed
more or less spontaneously and varies in its make-up from place
to place. At a country sale it will probably consist of a few local
antique dealers and junkmen, a runner or two and one or more
dealers from London or other cities. There will probably be nothing prearranged about their meeting, for each one will have been
hoping that he is going to be the only one at the sale. If it is a
particularly good sale they may meet on a viewing day prior to
the sale, otherwise they will not know until the actual morning
of the sale who is going to be there. One dealer can easily recognize another dealer even if they have never met before, and in a
very short time the fraternity will have come together to discuss
the pickings. The most important (financially) of them will become "chairman" by mutual consent, and another, probably a
local man who knows the auctioneer well, will be chosen to make
the ring's bids. All will agree on the maximum he shall bid for any
particular lot, but in fact the figure will more often than not be
determined by the "chairman." Since he is the most likely man to
get the property in the end, he will want to keep the bid as low as
possible, not only for the obvious reason but also because he does
not want to give away to his fellow ring men his true estimate of
the picture's value. If there are others as knowledgeable and as
prosperous as himself in the group he and they will form a ring
within the ring, for the proverbial honor among thieves does not
bother the experienced practitioner of ringmanship.

Having got the pictures they want, the members of the ring
leave the sale room for some place—a car, a pub, the premises of
a local man, etc.—where they can get down to the real business of
the day. The "chairman" now takes over the role of auctioneer

(an auctioneer with the right to bid for himself), and each picture is put up for sale again. This is called the knockout. The bidding begins at a little above the price paid for the lot in the sale room. Let us say, for example, that a picture has been bought for £100. The first bid is now £110, and the figure is raised in £10 bids to, say, £200, when the picture is knocked down by the auctioneer to himself or to one of the other more prosperous dealers. The buyer must now pay £100 (the difference between the sale room price and the knock down price), which is shared equally among all the other ring members. If, for example, there are nine members in the ring, eight of them now get £12 10s. each. Most of them are probably quite happy. It is quite likely that none of them could have afforded to buy the picture even at £100, so they have made £12 10s. for absolutely nothing—except a little bluff.

Now the riffraff have left the meeting place and there are, say, only three men left, the inner ring. By previous agreement two of them did not bid at all in the first knockout, but now there is a second knockout, in which it is each man for himself. This time the bidding starts at above £200 and probably goes up in much bigger leaps. It is likely that all three men know the true value of the picture, and it will probably be only their individual resources or knowledge of where they can sell it that determines who finally gets it. Let us now suppose that in this second knockout the price is £1,000. The successful bidder must now give the other two men £400 each. He is also responsible for settling with the sale room and, if he was not the buyer in the first knockout, reimbursing whoever paid the first shareout.*

The picture that was originally a £100 picture is now a £1,000 picture, but that is by no means the end. The new owner may now

---

* The description I have given is of a very simple operation. At times, when there is a large number of members in the ring, the knockout and the payout can be very complicated. For further details I recommend Geoffrey Johns's novel *Any Advance?*

have it cleaned, spend £50 on a good frame and sell it to a client, if he has any, at 100 or 200 per cent profit. More likely he will leave it as it is and take it straight to Sotheby's or Christie's, where he will ask for it to be sold with a reserve price (i.e., a price below which he is not prepared to part with it) which will ensure that he does not lose money on it and that no ring can possibly get it cheap. Reserve prices are the best protection there is against the rings. The bigger auctioneers always ask a vendor if he wishes to put a reserve price on his property and will give advice as to what it should be. That is why the rings' activities are so restricted in the major sale rooms. There are, however, many occasions, especially where property is being sold by order of executors of a will, in which reserve prices are waived. This is often the case with sales of the contents of private houses, and it is at the more important of these that the rings make their biggest killings.

The Auctions (Bidding Agreements) Act, which made rings illegal, was passed in 1927. It reads:

If any dealer agrees to give, or gives, or offers any gift or consideration to any other persons as an inducement or reward for abstaining, or for having abstained, from bidding at a sale by auction either generally or for any particular lot, or if any person agrees to accept, or accepts, or attempts to obtain from any such dealer any such gift or consideration as aforesaid, he shall be guilty of an offence under this Act, and shall be liable on summary conviction to a maximum penalty of six months' imprisonment and a fine of £100.

So far there has not been a single successful prosecution under the Act. The reason always given for this is that it is virtually impossible to prove that anyone has abstained from bidding. Even so, if a serious effort were made by the police in co-operation with the reputable auctioneers and dealers, something could be done to reduce the prevalence of this crime. In my own experience the ring men have become so bold that they might easily give them-

selves away to police officers masquerading as dealers. On one
occasion in a sale room I was sitting next to a dealer when another dealer, whom he knew only by sight, put a note into his
hands and walked away. The note said, "We are bidding for Lot
So-and-so. If you lay off we will settle with you afterwards." The
dealer, who had had no intention of bidding for Lot So-and-so,
did not know what to do. He was sufficiently intrigued by the
incident to want to find out what was meant by "we will settle
with you afterwards," but in the event the ring was outbid by
someone else and the occasion for settling did not arise. On another occasion, after I had outbid a hastily formed ring at a small
sale, I was approached by one of their number, who tried first
to sow doubt in my mind about the value of the lot and then
offered me a check for half the price I had paid in order to share
my risk of loss!

I have found that even those people in the art trade whose behavior is absolutely unimpeachable are reticent about discussing
the activities of the rings. It is as if they feared that by simply
admitting that they are aware of a ring's existence they will become contaminated. At the big auction houses they take the attitude that they do all they can to combat the ring with reserve
prices and accurate catalogue information and that, anyway, the
menace rarely shows itself in their sale rooms. But it does show
itself sometimes, especially in furniture and jewelry sales, and
even at Sotheby's and Christie's I have seen what were obviously
knockouts going on inside the buildings.

In November 1964 the *Sunday Times* caused something of a
sensation by exposing the activities of a ring of antique dealers
concerned in the buying of a superb Chippendale commode at a
Leamington Spa sale for £750—considerably less than a tenth of
its retail market value. But much more important than the actual
case quoted was the fact that the newspaper's staff showed that,
as I have suggested, successful police action under the 1927 act

would not have been impossible. If a *Sunday Times* reporter, armed with a pocket radio transmitter, was able to bluff his way into the knockout following a major country sale and relay the whole proceedings so that a tape recording could be made by his accomplices outside, surely the police could have done the same thing long before. From the general discussion that followed this brilliant newspaper investigation the most disturbing evidence that emerged was to the effect that in many cases the rings operate with the connivance of the country auctioneers. This connivance may go much deeper than is apparent in the sale room to the private buyer who finds his bids being ignored or who, after getting a lot knocked down to him, is told when he tries to collect it that he "must be mistaken, it is on a dealer's list." At Christie's and Sotheby's I have heard many reports of country auctioneers who, when called in to advise on the disposal of the contents of big houses, try to retain for sale in their own auction rooms property that would sell much better in a London auction room. At best this is the understandable fault of a businessman wanting to keep prestige and commission for himself. At worst it is a criminal betrayal, for gain—sometimes a very big gain—of his responsibility to the vendor.

In a case that was being freely talked about in the art trade a few years ago, a country auctioneer kept back a painting which he later knocked down to the ring at £30. In the ring's knockout it went, for a figure said to be around £2,000, to a dealer who then put it into a London auction room where it made more than £50,000.

In such a case as this a corrupt auctioneer would probably have to resort to some trick to ensure that only those dealers in league with him knew of the existence of the lot. One method is to omit the lot from the catalogue and then introduce it into the sale at the last moment as an "additional lot." Another is to omit it from the preview and tell enquirers that it has been temporarily withdrawn. Sometimes it may simply be hung in a dark and inaccessible position. I have been to sales at which the evidence suggested that all of these tricks were being employed either by the auctioneer or by a porter on his own initiative. A pound or a fiver slipped to a porter will often be enough to ensure that a particular lot is "lost" until the sale takes place. At one auction room I often visit I have found again and again that things I have gone to view are missing on preview days, but they always turn up on the day of the sale.

Even in London, at one of the smaller sale rooms, I had a very suspicious experience. What sounded like a £2,000 or £3,000 picture was listed in the catalogue of a sale composed otherwise of junk. I went to the sale room and, after searching in vain for the picture, was told by a porter that it had been withdrawn. I took his word for it and did not go to the sale, but afterward, out of curiosity, I phoned the auctioneer's office, gave the catalogue number of the "withdrawn" lot and asked how much it had fetched. When told that it had made fourteen pounds, I asked the clerk if it was the picture described in the catalogue and was assured that it was. Unfortunately I did not pursue the matter any further and am still left wondering what was behind this little mystery.

At the end of 1964 the *Sunday Times* exposé led to some dramatic repercussions inside the British Antique Dealer's Association, several of whose members had been involved in the "curious case of the Chippendale commode." (The newspaper had also revealed that four council members and twenty-seven ordinary members of the BADA had taken part in a second ring, at the sale of the effects of the late Captain E. G. "George" Spencer-Churchill, at Northwick Park, Gloucestershire, in September 1964.) After the president of the Association and about half of its thirty-two-man council had resigned, a new, smaller council was appointed and a new rule was made requiring all BADA members to sign a declaration that they would not take part in "knockout agreements." A few days later, on December 23, when rings were the subject of a debate in the House of Commons, there were cries of "Commercial brigandage!," "Crooks!" and "Parasites!" The rings were likened by enthusiastic M.P.s to the wartime black market and to slumlords. "The only way to kill these mosquitoes is to drain the swamp in which they breed," said Mr. Ridley (Conservative, Cirencester and Tewkesbury) with fine fervor but without (at least, so far as my newspaper reported him) defining exactly where or what the swamp was and how it was to be drained. The BADA was praised for "seeking to put its house in order," and its new president, Mr. Hugh Agnew, was commended for his remarkable courage and leadership "in combating this evil."

But pending the implementation of a Government promise to examine the question of bringing in new legislation on auction sales, rings have gone on more or less as before, even without the participation of BADA members. Any intention their operators may have had to act with more discretion has evidently been offset by rapacity born of the fear that their days may be numbered and the necessity of making as much hay as possible before the sun sets. And even now, in mid-1966, the public's only safeguard against the rings is still as it has always been, the reserve price. In London it is reasonably safe to take the auctioneer's advice on this matter, but in the country, where the auctioneer may be more accustomed to selling young heifers than Old Masters, it is advisable to get an independent expert's valuation of anything you may wish to sell that looks remotely like a work of art. Just how important this can be is illustrated by some of the stories of "discoveries" that are told in the next chapter.

8

Discoveries
and
How
to
Discover
Them

Whereas the millionaire and the rich man may, as things stand at present, form fine collections by sheer power of capital, the poor man has to depend on his wits. Yet the necessity which forces him to be his own expert is not altogether a hard necessity . . . Now and then he may snatch some treasure under the very eyes of dealers and millionaires, or may unearth in some grimy portfolio a drawing for which a fellow could hardly be found outside a royal or national collection.

—Sir Charles Holmes,
Pictures and Picture Collecting

One day way back in 1933 my friend Pierre Jeannerat, who was then twenty-one (and is now art critic of the *Daily Mail*), was looking around Christie's when he came across a wooden box containing a couple of bronze horses and two Victorian bronze cherubs. Idly picking them up one after the other, he realized that one of the horses was of a completely different quality from the other items in the job lot. It was squat and distorted and had nothing of the prettiness of the other horse, but somewhere in his memory it rang a bell. He studied it closely, holding it at different angles in his hands, until suddenly he realized what it was that it had evoked in his memory—Leonardo da Vinci's many drawings of rearing horses that he had seen at Windsor Castle, studies for *The Battle of Anghiari*, for *Saint George and the Dragon* and for the Trivulzio Monument. Hardly daring to hope that he had discovered a hitherto unknown bronze by the great Florentine master, he left the sale room and began a feverish search for every bit of information he could find about Leonardo's sculpture, and when the day of the sale arrived he was convinced that the horse was a study for the Trivulzio Monument. But had anyone else come to a similar conclusion? The tension as he waited for the lot number to be called was almost unbearable. He knew that if any dealer felt as he felt about the horse he could not hope to get it. The highest sum he could possibly afford to bid was fifty pounds, little more than the lot would be worth if all the bronzes were Victorian. He waited in an agony of suspense that justifies every cliché. The bidding started at one guinea, and at eleven and a half guineas the lot was knocked down—to him.

For years afterward he was almost alone in believing that his horse was by Leonardo, but slowly experts throughout the world began to consider his claim seriously, and in 1961 his faith in his own judgment was seen to be fully justified when the horse was included in the major exhibition of Italian bronze statuettes held at the Victoria and Albert Museum. It was listed as by Leonardo in the catalogue, which included this description of it by the eminent authority John Pope-Hennessy:

The statuette forms one of a group of three horses by or after Leonardo, of which the most celebrated is a Riding Warrior at Budapest and the second is in the Metropolitan Museum of Art, New York. The horses are the only works of sculpture that can be directly associated with Leonardo, and certainly depend from models by this artist. It has been claimed that both the present bronze and that at Budapest are preparatory studies for Leonardo's Trivulzio Monument, but, as noted by Clark, their closest affinities in Leonardo's work are with the drawings for the fresco of the Battle of Anghiari, and it is likely that they are casts from wax models for the fresco by Leonardo, and were made in Florence *c.* 1508.

The story of Jeannerat's horse (which, incidentally, is probably worth at least £100,000 today) is of the sort that makes us all ask ourselves, "Why can't I find a masterpiece?" If we are to judge by newspaper reports, one such discovery is made almost every day. "Painting in Cupboard May Be an Art Treasure," "£1 Picture Is a Rembrandt," "Cleaned-up Painting May Be Worth £100,000" read the headlines, but nine times out of ten no more is heard about these spectacular finds. The late Sir Albert Richardson, a former president of the Royal Academy and therefore a man who ought to have known better, repeatedly made news with reports of his sensational discoveries. I have no doubt he did find many worthwhile pictures, for he was knowledgeable about art and an assiduous explorer of junk and antique shops, but wishful thinking, the archenemy of true scholarship, played far too big a part in his searches and research. He relied entirely upon his own judgment and was contemptuous of that of others who disagreed with him.

Once when I went to see him at his home in Ampthill he had just discovered a new "Gainsborough," a version of the National Gallery's famous picture of the artist's daughters chasing a butterfly. When I dared to suggest that it could be a good Victorian copy he said, "It's the Victorian frame. Fooled everybody, but not me." Had he, I asked, taken it to the National Gallery for verification? "It's not safe there," he joked (it was shortly after the Goya theft at the Gallery). I was taken on a conducted tour of the house, which was like an antique shop in which the good and the indifferent jostled on equal terms. He was like Aladdin in the magic cave. He opened a door and exclaimed, "There's Mrs.

Fitzherbert by Gainsborough! And look at those: Constable, Wouwerman, Greuze, Hogarth—he painted it in an hour for a bet —and Vernet, an original Vernet! And there! An Egg! And that— Swebach *dit* Fontaine, the only one in England! Oh, and look at our dear friend Ford Madox Brown under a Teniers. And see those? Rubens, Fisher Prout and Rushbury all together!" Then he dashed ahead to another room and started the spiel all over again. "That's a van Goyen and this is a Claude. Here's a Wilson and this is Benjamin West's *St. James's Park*. Chardin, Opie, Girtin, a very early Constable, Lépine, Cundall—it all mixes, see?"

After my comments on the "Gainsborough" I was given no opportunity to study any of the other pictures closely to see if they all justified Sir Albert's enthusiasm. But two months after my visit the following newspaper reports appeared:

Sir Albert Goes Nap

He has done it again! For the fifth time in six months Professor Sir Albert Richardson has identified an unknown picture as a valuable work by a great artist.

The 81-year-old professor went to lunch with my colleague Jimmy Wentworth Day, gazed at a picture on the dining-room wall and announced: "You've got a genuine Reynolds there."

He was right.

How does it happen that Sir Albert has found quite so many pictures lately?

"Oh, I don't know," he said with a shrug. "But I haven't been collecting pictures for sixty years for nothing, you know."

Tomorrow the picture, *The Education of Love,* goes up for sale at Sotheby's.

"I'm hoping for a five-figure sum," says Wentworth Day. The picture has been in his family for many years, but its painter has remained a mystery until now.

—Daily Mail, January 30, 1962

UNSOLD PICTURE

It must have been disappointing for the owner of the picture attributed to Reynolds when it failed to find a buyer at Sotheby's this week and was bought in for £30.

But the man who spotted it as a Reynolds, Sir Albert Richardson— that architect with a flair for finding Old Masters—is not perturbed. The picture is a copy of a painting by Titian, and Sir Albert tells me it is of no great value.

"It is one of a number of sketches Reynolds did as a student in Italy," says Sir Albert. "But it is unquestionably by Reynolds. It came from Wentworth Woodhouse and had been in the owner's family for years."

—*Evening Standard,* February 3, 1962

What both stories omitted to say was that Sotheby's did not by any means agree that the picture was "unquestionably by Reynolds." It was catalogued as "Reynolds," which, as we have seen in Chapter Five, means it is almost certainly *not* by dear old Sloshy Slosh (as his less respectful students used to call him).

Another collector of this somewhat eccentric kind was Captain George Spencer-Churchill. A cultured and erudite man, he too preferred to be his own expert and "authenticated" his own pictures. He was a great believer in his own hunches and almost invariably bought dirty pictures, pictures so obscured by old varnish and grime that no one could say with any certainty whom they were by. But Spencer-Churchill claimed that if he could see a single blade of grass he could tell the quality of the picture, and on the strength of that he would buy or not buy. In this way he added about two hundred pictures, which he called "Northwick Rescues," to that part of the great Northwick collection which he had inherited. Of the two hundred a few were very good finds —Dirck Bouts's *Madonna and Child,** a flower piece by Nicolas

---

* It fetched £15,750 when sold at Christie's in May 1965.

van Verendael (only an ear of corn was visible when he bought it) and a fine portrait of Queen Elizabeth of Bohemia (the Winter Queen) by an unknown English artist of the early sixteenth century. There was also a painting of a woman, said to be by Dürer, in which the face had been damaged beyond restoration, so Captain Spencer-Churchill had a new face painted in. The artist he chose to do it was James Gunn, R.A.!

By the law of averages (or some such), if a collector buys enough pictures in the right places he is bound to acquire some good things. But for most of us this rich man's method is out of the question. Yet even for people without much money and without any specialized knowledge of painting or sculpture it is still possible to find "Jeannerat horses." The secret is, I believe, taste. (I say this in spite of the fact that "taste" *in an artist* is inimical to great art.) It may be simply a general taste for what is good in art or a specialized taste for the unusual. In either case it can be acquired—just as a taste for good wine can be acquired, only more cheaply. That is what museums and art galleries are for. Anyone who regularly frequents such places as the National Gallery and the Victoria and Albert Museum and really looks at the things there will unconsciously develop a feeling for quality.

Two items in the same sale at Sotheby's in October 1963 illustrated how valuable a thing taste, in these instances a taste for the exotic, can be. The first item, a Mexican-looking carved stone mask, had been bought by a Kent policeman for four pounds in a bookshop; Sotheby's recognized it as an early work of Henry Moore and sold it on behalf of the policeman's wife for £1,000. The second item had also been picked up in a bookshop (where it was serving as a paperweight), for half a crown; it turned out to be a Negro-influenced bronze by the sculptor Henri Gaudier-Brzeska, and it fetched £160. In November 1964 the Victoria and Albert Museum bought a gold-decorated bronze figure of a man for £4,000 from a London antique dealer who had bought it for

£16 in a village auction in Kent. There were thirty-two other dealers at the sale, but none of them took any notice of the bronze, which proved to be a characteristic piece by the late-Renaissance sculptor Antico. The dealer who bought it confessed that he had no special knowledge of Italian bronzes. But although the figure's finer points were concealed by grime when he first saw it, there was something about it that appealed to his taste, a taste developed unconsciously through years of looking at and handling good things.

Most of the stories I hear about discoveries of this sort, however, confirm my belief that the enormous growth of interest in art that we hear so much about is, for the most part, only an interest in the *price* of art. Promoted and fed by newspaper reports, this interest has led hordes of hopefuls to take "Grandmother's painting" to Bond Street and King Street. Among them was the man who took a little oil painting on panel, that had been knocking around his home for years, into the office at Sotheby's and asked, "Is this worth a fiver?" When told it was an early Samuel Palmer, a remarkable example of the artist's "visionary period," he replied, "I know it's a Samuel Palmer. He gave it to my grandmother. But is it worth a fiver?" It sold for £5,600. Two other Samuel Palmers, water colors, which sold in 1964 for £1,000 and £2,500, belonged to a man who had acquired them with the contents of a shooting lodge he had bought in Scotland. He thought they were prints until an art-student friend put him wise.

There are endless stories of this sort: the woman who bought a £2,100 Krieghoff at a jumble sale for half a crown; the Stock Exchange clerk who found that the two water colors Aunt Ethel had given him for his wedding twenty years earlier were by Alexander Cozens and, although damp-stained after serving for years as lagging for the tanks in his loft, fetched £550 and £200; the laborer who, fifteen years after buying some old pictures at a country auction, discovered in 1962 that one of them was by

Claude Lorrain and sold it to Birmingham Art Gallery at the bargain price of £4,400; and, oddest of all, the noble lord who, having failed to sell one of his many old paintings for thirty shillings in a charity bazaar, took it to Sotheby's, who sold it—as a Rubens —for £32,000. In all these cases, it will be noted, the vendors were apparently without any knowledge of art, and chance played a great part in their good fortune. It makes one shudder to think how many masterpieces have perished or been lost through the ignorance of their owners.

Even since I began writing this book dozens more such "discoveries" have been reported. The most intriguing of these concerned a miniature bought in a £12 lot of pictures at the sale of the contents of a bungalow in Nottinghamshire. The buyer, a former London policeman turned market-gardener-cum-art-dealer, sent the miniature to Christie's, where it was identified as a miniature commissioned from Peter Oliver by Charles I in 1630. It is a copy of a *Holy Family* by Correggio which has been missing since the Civil Wars. The whereabouts of the miniature, which is the only record of the Correggio, was unknown from the time it was painted until 1964. At Christie's, not very long ago, it was sold for 820 guineas. In the same month, at Sotheby's, a very different sort of find, two forgotten stone carvings by Henry Moore, turned up. They came from the garden of a house in Wimbledon that had been bought three years earlier by the famous viola player Lionel Tertis. A curious feature here was that the house had once been advertised for sale "complete with garden sculptures by Henry Moore," but Mr. Tertis had not seen the advertisements. It was only after he had been in the house for some time that he learned that they might be by Moore and invited the sculptor to look at them. The two heavy blocks of stone had been carved in 1928 and were considerably weathered, but they fetched £5,200.

Belonging to a different class of discovery, one in which specialized knowledge plays a big part, was the fine Rembrandt still life which was sold at Sotheby's in June 1964 for £110,000. It had been bought at a sale in a Midlands mansion for less than a hundred pounds by a London dealer who had detected the master's touch under the layers of dark-brown varnish and dirt. This is the sort of coup the amateur picture sleuth dreams of, but the pleasures of the hunt are no less exciting where the rewards are far less spectacular. Of the many bargains I have bought, none has given me more pleasure than the first—a charming small canal scene, by William Williams (Williams of Norwich), for which I paid three-and-sixpence in the Portobello Road when I was very young and which is now worth perhaps forty or fifty pounds. It was one of a pair, but I had enough money for only one. On my way home to get another three-and-six I met a friend, showed him the picture and told him where I got it. By the time I returned to the shop he had been in and bought the second picture. There is, of course, a moral in this: Never tell a friend what you are doing in the art game or you may lose a picture—and a friend.

One has only to have a small taste of success like this to become a compulsive junk-shop addict. This can be great fun, but it is also a great time-waster. The true addict can never go anywhere straight from A to B, and even on a Sunday he will leave his wife fuming in the car while he peers through the windows of closed shops. The only cure is satiety and the realization that there are millions and millions of pictures in the world and the vast majority of them are worthless. It then dawns on him that it is stupid to search hundreds of places in which he may find a few pictures when he can, in fact, go to a few places that have hundreds of pictures—the auction rooms. By then, too, it will have dawned on him that junk shops are not what they used to be, that most junk men today are shrewd men who, although they may not share his frankness, certainly share the feelings of the dealer in Chelsea who displayed in his window a sign that read: "Member of the Society for the Protection of Junk-Men. No professional or amateur art dealers wanted nor any other members of the public who are trying to grind junk-dealers down." When you went into this gentleman's shop he would appear, looking very sinister, at the top of a flight of stairs and announce, "You won't find anything there. I've got all the good stuff safe up here and I'm keeping it." And it was no use trying the old I-was-only-looking-for-frames gambit. "Yes," he used to say, "they all say that." It could be very embarrassing if you really were looking for frames.

The chapter that follows is intended as an introduction to the auction rooms. It is meant for the sort of timid creature (I know he exists, because he is always telling me about his fears) who is afraid to go to an auction—especially one at Sotheby's or Christie's —in case the auctioneer thinks he is bidding when in fact he is only breathing. It is also meant for the tyro art-gamesman and is offered with a warning that, although auctioneers are dealt with before dealers in this book, he will be wise to learn all he can from and about dealers before he starts nodding and winking at auctioneers.

9
The
Shotgun
Wedding

> *If you go into a dealer's you can
> see something, consider it and
> then ask your wife and your aunt
> what they think of it. But in the
> sale room a revolver is put to your
> head. It's now or never. It's a sort
> of shotgun wedding.*
>
> —PETER WILSON,
> CHAIRMAN OF SOTHEBY'S,
> in an interview on the
> BBC Third Programme

In recent years the activities of the art market have been given almost as much prominence in the press as sporting events, and big sales at Sotheby's or Christie's have filled as many column inches as boxing matches. It was not always so. It is a postwar phenomenon, and even as late as the mid-1950s the big auctioneers and the general public remained virtually unaware of each other's existence. Outstandingly high prices paid in the sale rooms had, of course, always rated a few lines down the news pages of the daily papers, but these served only to stress the remoteness of the world of art money from the ordinary newspaper reader. Fine-art auctioneers cared little for publicity of a popular sort. Although they had been disposing of art for money since the eighteenth century, both Christie's and Sotheby's preferred to be thought of as art institutions rather than market places. And since only a minute and elite fraction of the public was interested in buying works of art it seemed to them that there was nothing to be gained by having their affairs bandied about. They therefore treated the popular press with a couldn't-care-less coolness that continued until 1958, when they made a complete *volte-face* and began to woo newspapers, magazines, radio and television with all the ardor that modern public-relations methods can simulate.

Why 1958? That was the year of the phenomenal Goldschmidt sale, in which just seven Impressionist and Post-Impressionist pictures were sold at Sotheby's for £781,000. It was also the year in which Peter Wilson became chairman of the firm. Although still little loved and largely unwooed, the popular press showed tremendous interest in the Goldschmidt sale. The "madness" of people who would spend such vast sums of money on pictures, and modern pictures at that, was a fitting subject even for those who had never heard of Cézanne or Manet, Renoir or van Gogh. Never before had any sale—and with it the name of Sotheby's—been so widely talked about.

The new chairman, whose pained remark as he brought down the hammer on the £220,000 Cézanne, "Will nobody bid any more?," established him as art-gamesman number one, saw this as a propitious moment at which to set about changing the firm's public image. He must have perceived that publicity of the most general sort can whip up that covetousness which (as he has since pointed out) works so virulently upon the hearts, minds and purse strings of collectors. And he must have recognized that the new style of collector welcomes publicity, that in fact what he is collecting is not pictures but self-aggrandizement.

Publicity, then, even of the most popular sort, was seen to be good for business and was therefore to be encouraged. But there was a problem. Although newspaper editors had fallen over themselves to give the story of a three-quarters-of-a-million-pound sale they were unlikely to be impressed by anything less spectacular in the future unless it was presented to them in a very "newsworthy" form. So it came about that in 1959 Sotheby's appointed a firm of press and public-relations experts to keep their name in front of the public on television and radio and in every branch of the press. The outcome has been as phenomenal as the Goldschmidt sale itself. The effect of triumphs in the sale room and publicity triumphs following one upon the other almost continuously has made London the undisputed center of the world art market. Millions of pounds' worth of works of art from other countries, especially in the Americas, are sent to London to be sold every year. In Britain the name Sotheby has become a household world in even the meanest household. It is a synonym for art at fantastic prices, and yet (and that is the most remarkable and, from the point of view of this book, the most interesting outcome of all the publicity) the image of the firm is no longer unreal to the man in the rush-hour bus or tube train. In the last few years thousands of people who in the past would have been too overawed to set foot inside the Bond Street sale room have gone there to watch, to buy or, most commonly, to sell. Thus a largely new source of considerable income was brought to light—the sale of great quantities of properties from vendors of modest means to buyers of modest means. During the 1964–65 season at Sotheby's (and Christie's had a similar experience) no less than 76 per cent of all lots sold went for £ 100 or less and 30 per cent for £ 25 or less.

Every day now a procession of optimists, their enthusiasm fired by accounts of fortunes made in the sale rooms, may be seen, with brown-paper parcels under their arms, converging on the offices of the big auctioneers. As they go in their hopes are high. Soon

they will come out with them confirmed or shattered or just
brought down to earth. Let us imagine that you are one of them
and see what happens.

Your brown-paper parcel contains that dark old flower painting
that has been hanging over your mantlepiece unnoticed for
twenty or thirty years. You know it is old because it belonged to
your mother and your grandmother before you. It is at least a
hundred years old, so it must be worth quite a bit, you think (but
it does not follow). Perhaps it is worth thousands. You have read
in the papers recently about a flower piece by someone called
van Huysum that sold for £5,000 and another by another Dutch-
can called van der Ast that fetched over £10,000. But no, you
won't even hope for so much, even a few hundreds would be
nice. Anyway, there is no harm in asking. You undo your parcel
and show the picture to a girl at the reception desk. She knows
little more about painting than you do, but she says, "I'll get
someone from the Old-Master Department to look at it if you will
just wait a moment."

You wait. Already your hopes are soaring. The Old-Master Department? So it's an Old Master! You are not quite sure what
"an Old Master" means, but you have an idea that all Old Masters
are worth a lot of money, even more than Impressionists. You take
another look at the picture. Why didn't you see before that it is
very beautiful? Look at all the marvelous detail in those leaves!
And that ladybird, it looks absolutely lifelike. Your thoughts are
interrupted by the arrival of a man from the Old Master department who looks far too well-dressed and young to be an expert.

"Good morning," he says and glances at your picture. "You
want us to sell this for you?"

"Well, I . . . er . . ." you stammer. "I wondered if you could
tell me what it is."

"Oh yes," he says. "It's very nice. A late one, but attractive." He

takes it over to a light and looks at it more closely for a few seconds and returns. "It's in good condition, should clean up well."

"You mean I should have it cleaned?" you ask.

"Oh no. If you want us to sell it, leave it as it is. Makes it more
intriguing to the buyer. Anyway, the dealers like the dirt—it hides
the quality of the picture from the nonexpert."

"I see," you say, and then, feeling rather a fool for not knowing
the answer yourself, you ask, "Can you tell me whom it is by?"

The young man glances at it again. "Well, no, I can't say more
than that it's late eighteenth century. But we will be able to give
it a name," he adds cryptically.

Then you buck up courage to ask the question that has been
uppermost in your mind for days. "Any idea how much it is
worth?" you say with feigned casualness.

The young man, who even in his few years at Sotheby's has
seen scores, even hundreds, of Dutch flower pieces of this period
and quality sold, answers immediately, "Four to five hundred
pounds."

You don't know whether to be pleased or disappointed. Even
four hundred pounds was much more than you had hoped for
when you first took the picture off the wall, but since then you
have dreamed of thousands. But you hide your emotions and tell
the young man that you will leave it to be sold. He gives you a
receipt, tells you that it will probably be sold in two or three
months' time and that a catalogue will be sent to you in good time
for you to decide what reserve you wish to put on your picture.
You go home and try to forget about it, until the day the catalogue drops through your letterbox.

Attached to the catalogue is a form that tells you your picture
is Lot No. So-and-so. You turn up Lot No. So-and-so and read:
"Van Huysum—Roses, Delphiniums, Mallow and other flowers in
an urn on a stone ledge, with a ladybird and a caterpillar, 26 in.
by 19 in." You are very excited. So it is by van Huysum! Or is it?

You suddenly remember what you have read in Chapter Five of this book about methods of cataloguing. "Van Huysum" means simply that the auctioneers have decided that it is in the manner of that artist, probably by an imitator or follower of his, possibly a copy of one of his pictures, but not by the master himself. There is, of course, still a slender chance that they may be wrong and that other experts, among the dealers, may believe that it is by van Huysum himself and will compete for it at the sale. Perhaps you ought to have shown it to one or two other experts before deciding to sell. You could, for example, have taken it to the National Gallery for an opinion free of charge or had it valued by a professional valuer. Even now you could withdraw it from the sale, but that would not make you very popular with the auctioneers. You decide, instead, to telephone the young expert you saw at the auctioneer's and discuss with him what reserve price you are going to put on it. Would £400 be about right? you ask. The young man thinks it is too high, suggests three hundred. This depresses you a bit again. Has he gone cold on your picture? No, he just wants to be reasonably certain that it does sell. So do you, but you don't want to give it away. You make a compromise—at £350.

A few days before the sale is due, your picture and all the others in "your" sale (as you have now come to think of it) are put on view. You go along to have a look. It takes some time to find your picture, it looks so much smaller now than it looked at home and they have not hung it in the best possible position. In fact, you begin to wonder if anyone will notice it at all. You find there are two more flower pieces in the sale. One, much smaller than yours and not nearly so pretty (it's all sort of stiff and flattish), is catalogued as by "Balthasar van der Ast." The second one is very much like yours but considerably bigger and is catalogued as by "Jan van Huysum." As far as you can see it is not in any way better than yours—well, only very slightly, anyway—so why didn't they catalogue yours with the artist's name in full? You have a good mind to ask the young man why. In fact, you do ask him, and he explains very courteously. In the first place the big picture is signed and dated (1740), it comes from an important collection, and its history during all but the first twenty or thirty years of its existence is documented. But what is even more important is that the drawing, the design, the color and the almost miraculous precision of the painting announce immediately that it is the work of a master and that master is Jan van Huysum.

The young man puts your picture alongside the big one, and for a moment you too can see that there is a difference. What you thought was the marvelous detail in your picture is not now quite so marvelous. The color is not so rich or varied as that in the bigger picture, the design is not so intricate, and the paint surface is not nearly so well preserved. In fact, says the young man, your picture was painted at least fifty years after the other one, and forty years after van Huysum's death, when there was a vogue for his pictures and they were fetching very high prices. It was probably painted as an honest imitation of a style that was in demand, but it might have been done as a fake van Huysum—it hardly matters now. It is just a very nice flower piece by an unknown late-eighteenth- or early-nineteenth-century artist.

On the day of the sale you arrive early and find yourself a seat where you can see as much as possible of what is going on. A quarter of an hour before the sale is due to start you are still almost alone in the sale room and are beginning to worry that nobody is going to be at the sale to buy your picture. Ten minutes later the room has filled up and the only seats empty are reserved ones. Most of them are reserved for the dealers, who arrive with only a minute or two to spare. They are mostly well-dressed, indistinguishable from any other sort of businessmen, not at all arty. They have a slightly arrogant air, an air of self-importance like that of theater critics at a first night. They talk and laugh together like the best of friends, but soon their quips and cranks will give way to wanton wiles, nods and becks, and, maybe, wreathèd smiles. They are still talking when, precisely at the published time, the auctioneer climbs onto his rostrum and announces without any preamble, "Lot One." A porter holds the lot up to him for inspection and then shows it to the audience.

"Lot One. Ten pounds?" asks the auctioneer. But no one wants to be the first bidder. "Five pounds, then?" he asks, and then, as someone signals a bid, he adds, "Five pounds is bid." Now the bids follow fast upon each other. "Eight. Ten. Twelve. Fifteen. Eighteen. Twenty. . . . Twenty pounds. Twenty-five. Thirty. . . ." Finally Lot One, in which no one seemed interested enough to offer £10 at the start, is knocked down for £90. And you have learned your first lesson: Never let your rivals (or the auctioneer) see how anxious you are to get a particular lot. Sometimes at the smaller sale rooms an excited novice, impatient with an auctioneer who is raising the bidding ten shillings at a time, will call out much higher bids and so alert others to the fact that he thinks he is on to a good thing. At other times the overanxious bidder finds he is bidding against himself, and the auctioneer has to tell him, "It's your bid, sir."

Although it may appear to you that the way in which the auctioneer raises the bids is entirely arbitrary, there is usually some method in it. In practice there are no hard and fast rules and the skillful auctioneer will be constantly adapting his method from lot to lot in such a way as to get the best possible price. Two main factors govern him: the price he hopes and aims to get and the price at which the bidding starts. If the first bid for Lot One in "your" sale had been £10, then the auctioneer would probably have continued raising the price in £10 units and sold it for the same final figure in rather shorter time. But if at some point no £10 bid was forthcoming, the auctioneer would have accepted a smaller advance.

One of the conditions of sale printed in the catalogues of most reputable auctioneers concerns the minimum advance that will be accepted. The wording varies. At Sotheby's it is: "No person to advance less than 5s.; above ten pounds 10s.; and so on in proportion, or at the Auctioneer's discretion." At Christie's: "No person to advance less than 1s.; above Five Pounds, 5s.; and so on in proportion." At Bonham's (London): "No person to advance less than 5|-.; above Ten Pounds, 10|-.; and so on in proportion (i.e., a 5% increase)." Phillips, Son & Neale (also in London) say only: "The Auctioneer may regulate the bidding," while Parke-Bernet, Sotheby's New York branch, reserve the right of the auctioneer to reject any advance that "is not of sufficient amount."

The references to advances of five shillings at Sotheby's and one shilling at Christie's are anachronisms; no lot at either house is ever offered at less than a pound, and no advances of less than that sum are accepted. But in general the five-per-cent-minimum-advance condition is applied. Occasionally when bids of tens of thousands of pounds are being made an auctioneer may refuse any advance of less than a thousand. Ultimately, however, the discretion of the auctioneer is what counts, and it pays to study him and learn his ways. Peter Wilson once told me the secret of being a good auctioneer: "You have to get your audience's confidence and then dominate them—in the nicest possible way, of course." But as a prospective buyer you must not allow yourself to be dominated, not even in the nicest possible way. Your aims and those of the auctioneer are directly opposed. During the sale he is temporarily the "enemy," and the more you understand about him the less likely you are to be afraid of him or to be carried away by his charm, eloquence, cunning or whatever is his particular weapon. When you know him well you will often be able to tell from his manner if you are bidding against a reserve and at what point the reserve has been passed, or whether a lot knocked down has really been sold or has been bought in. (The value of this sort of knowledge we shall see later.)

Usually the first few lots at any sale are comparatively unimportant items, and your sale is no exception. None of the first dozen lots fetches more than a few hundred pounds, but then comes a group of better things headed "The Property of a Lady of Title." Among them is the little flower piece by Balthasar van der Ast. "Lot ———," announces the auctioneer, "the flower painting by Balthasar van der Ast." He consults his catalogue and then says, "I have several bids. I must say two thousand five hundred pounds to start." You can hardly believe it. Two thousand five hundred for that little thing that, in your eyes, is not nearly as attractive as your own picture? "Two thousand five hundred, two thousand eight hundred, three thousand, three thousand five hundred, four thousand, four thousand five hundred, five thousand, five thousand five hundred," intones the auctioneer, looking first here, first there, without pausing. All the time you are scanning the audience, trying to make out who is bidding, but you can see no sign. "Five thousand five hundred pounds," he repeats and then, after a short pause, "Six thousand." That time you did see the bidder. Or, rather, you saw one of those men you took to be dealers raise his eyebrows to the auctioneer. "Six thousand five hundred." You did not see that one, because it came from the back of the room. But now the eyebrows are raised again. "Seven thousand." The auctioneer looks at the back of the room. Then to the dealer he says, "Seven thousand five hundred." Again the dealer raises his eyebrows, and it is £8,000. Another bid from the back of the room, and it is £8,500. The dealer hesitates. "Eight thousand five hundred. Against you," the auctioneer says to him. This time the dealer leaves his eyebrows where they are and says quietly, "And two." It is less than the required five per cent advance, but the auctioneer, who senses that the limit has been reached, accepts it. "Eight thousand seven hundred pounds."

He takes a last look round his audience, repeats, "At eight thousand seven hundred, then," brings down his hammer and says the buyer's name for the benefit of his clerk.

Now you are very excited. And rightly so, for that was a very good price (considerably more than the dealer, who knows he can sell it for 10,500 guineas, had wanted to pay). It was also a "textbook" piece of auctioneering to which there was more than met your eye. In the first place the "lady of title" was not willing to sell at less than £4,800 and had put a reserve price of that amount on the picture. Then three prospective buyers, who were presumably unable to be at the sale, had made advance bids (Americans call them "order bids") verbally or by letter or telegram. One of them was for a sum below the reserve, a second was for £5,200 and a third was for £6,500. The auctioneer was therefore sure, before the sale began, that the picture would be sold and that it would sell for at least £5,500—i.e., the amount of the highest advance bidder's first bid above the second advance bidder's limit.

In spite of this the auctioneer began the bidding at only £2,500. Being something of a psychologist (as well as a bit of an actor), he reasoned that to begin at £5,200, or even £5,500, as he could fairly have done, might have an adverse effect on some bidders. He knew, too, that he could excite his audience by a rush of bids rising to more than £5,000 in a matter of seconds, and that such excitement can affect bidders favorably from his point of view. But there was a third reason for starting at a comparatively low figure. Imagine that you had made an advance bid of, say, three or four thousand pounds and that you had, after all, been able to attend the sale, what would you have thought if the bidding had begun at a figure higher than your offer? Exactly. So the auctioneer made sure not only that justice was done but also that it was seen to be done. When, as you noticed, he paused at £5,500 he had reached the figure at which the man who had made an advance bid of "up to £6,500" would have got the picture if there had been no further bids from people present in the sale room. But, as you saw, there were several.

It may seem odd to you that the auctioneer should have accepted several advance bids one of which made it certain that none of the others could be successful. But this is a reflection of the strict confidence which is exercised where such bids are concerned. A reputable auctioneer will not reveal to an enquirer either the reserve price or the size of any bids already received. He will give an estimate of what the picture will sell for, and this will, of course, take into account the reserve price. In the case of the van der Ast the estimate given to anyone who asked was "rather more than six thousand." The final figure, a considerable surprise to the auctioneer and the owner, was brought about by rivalry between two dealers each of whom intended to sell it to the same collector.

Now back to the sale, where the van Huysum picture is about to be sold. The bidding starts at only £500 (there are no advance bids, and, although you think the picture is much more attractive than the last one, van Huysum is over a hundred years later than van der Ast and does not rate so highly in the market), goes up in £100 units to £1,000 and then in £200 units to £2,000. Again you can see no one bidding, but apparently the auctioneer can. He looks first in your direction, but above your head, and then at the clerk. You look behind you (unaware that sale room etiquette forbids it) but can see nobody there, and the awful thought strikes you that he may think *you* are bidding. You sit rigidly still, hardly daring to breathe. You watch the clerk, who is staring straight in front of him. He too is motionless, yet the auctioneer turns to him at every alternate bid. "Four thousand," says the auctioneer over your head, and then to the clerk, "Four thousand two hundred." The clerk continues to look straight ahead but then, after a moment, shakes his head. "At four thousand two hundred," says the auctioneer. He no longer looks over your head, but scans the whole audience and repeats the figure. Then, hesitantly, he taps his hammer, says something that sounds like Finkelbaum or Hogginbotham and proceeds to the next lot. You look behind you again, but there is no one who looks anything like a Finkelbaum or even a Hogginbotham. What has been going on?

Briefly it is this: The picture has been bought in, because it did not reach the reserve of £4,500 put on it by the owner against the auctioneer's advice. Finkelbaum or Hogginbotham (or whatever the auctioneer said) was a buying-in name for this sale (different names are used on different days). Each time the auctioneer looked over your head he was "taking one off the wall"—pretending to take a bid from the nonexistent Finkelbaum or Hogginbotham. If, as in this case, there is only one "real" bidder for a picture, the auctioneer will bid in this way until the reserve price is reached. In effect he is bidding for the owner of the picture, to ensure that it is not sold below the minimum price stipulated. (To be able to detect when a picture has been bought in can sometimes prove profitable to a dealer or collector. A disappointed would-be vendor is often ready, immediately after the sale, to accept a bargain price offered through the auctioneers.) The one "real" bidder this time was the auctioneer's clerk. If you had watched his hands instead of his face you would have seen that he signaled to the auctioneer by moving one finger almost imperceptibly. The clerk is frequently asked by clients who cannot get to the sale to bid on their behalf. In this case, however, the client was present, standing at the back of the room. He had arranged that the clerk of the sale should go on bidding for him until he gave a prearranged signal that meant "Stop." The signal? The removal of his spectacles.

Some people may adopt this surreptitious method of bidding just for the hell of it, but for those who, for some reason or other, do not wish to be seen bidding it is better than placing a fixed-limit bid with the auctioneer. Sometimes clients make such arrangements direct with the auctioneer. One important collector, for example, used to clasp his umbrella in front of him for as long as he was bidding and then let it slip through his fingers to show that he was giving up. Another would blow his nose to show that he was in the bidding and then blow it again to withdraw.

There are obviously dangers for the bidder in this sort of thing, as was discovered by the woman who, having arranged to take off her left glove when she had finished bidding, found that the glove had caught on her engagement ring. It can also put a great strain on the auctioneer, as was demonstrated sensationally at Christie's in March 1965 when Rembrandt's lovely portrait of his son Titus was sold—but only after a dispute—for a British sale room record price of £798,000. On that dramatic occasion I found myself, by chance, right next to Mr. Norton Simon, the American canned-food tycoon who bought the picture, and I had a close-up of exactly what happened.

For the first hour and a half of the sale Mr. Simon sat watching the proceedings and occasionally asking his neighbor, London art dealer Dudley Tooth, questions about the pictures and the prices. I took him to be an American tourist sight-seeing in the sale room and was surprised when he began to bid for Lot 101, Hogarth's *A Family Party*, the first of five pictures from the famous Cook collection, of which the Rembrandt was the most important. Mr. Simon made nearly all his bids by calling out "Five hundred" (500 guineas), thus drawing attention to himself and to the fact that he was not wholly familiar with the normal procedure in British sale rooms. When the bidding has passed 20,000 guineas it is usual for the auctioneer to raise the bidding by at least 1,000 guineas at a time, but Mr. Simon went on with his calls of "Five hundred" until even the 30,000-guinea mark was left behind. Even so he failed to get the picture, which went to Colnaghi's at 38,000 guineas (£39,900). In view of his subsequent statement that he wanted to avoid publicity until the Rembrandt was cleared for export to America, his behavior was inexplicable. The newspapermen were immediately interested in him and were watching him closely when the Rembrandt came up four lots later.

"Lot One Hundred and Five. One hundred thousand guineas offered," said the auctioneer, Christie's chairman Mr. I. O. ("Peter") Chance. The bidding leaped up, first in twenty-thousands, then fifty-thousands, and reached half a million in less than thirty seconds. Then Mr. Simon, who had been bidding openly by raising a finger and nodding his head, called out excitedly, "Six hundred thousand!" and the auctioneer came straight back with "And fifty." At that stage there were still at least four prospective buyers in the running. Dealer Geoffrey Agnew was sitting a few rows behind Mr. Simon, and as the American forced the pace he countered all his bids with discreet, almost imperceptible nods. But his interest ended at 700,000 guineas. Mr. Simon indicated one more bid, 720,000 guineas, and then remembered belatedly that he wanted to remain anonymous. So, when a counterbid of 740,-000 guineas came from the Duke of Beaufort's heir, David Somerset, acting for his firm, Marlborough Fine Art, Mr. Simon sat tight and said nothing. (Someone later affirmed that he was winking at the auctioneer, but this was never confirmed.)

For long seconds the auctioneer looked meaningful looks at Mr. Simon and Mr. Simon looked meaningful looks back at him, but neither got the other's meaning. "Any more? More? Bidding?" asked Mr. Chance, who was clearly reluctant to knock the picture down. "It's against you," he said, leaning over the edge of his rostrum toward Mr. Simon. When no reply came from the American the auctioneer surveyed the rest of the room, repeated, "Seven hundred and forty thousand guineas" and "Any more?" again and again, then rapped his little gavel and announced, "Marlborough Fine Art."

Immediately there was pandemonium. Spontaneous applause clashed with cries of anguish from Mr. Simon, "I am still bidding!" The smile of triumph died on Mr. Chance's face. Above the noise he called down to the American, "I said quite clearly it was against you." And of course we all knew that he had. But Mr. Simon was jumping mad. "You got my message, Mr. Chance," he shouted back. "You had definite instructions what to watch for." Mr. Chance looked baffled and shrugged his shoulders. "All right," said Mr. Simon, pulling a piece of paper out of his pocket, "I will read what it says here." In fact he first gave the paper to Mr. Tooth to read out, but when the dealer was unable to make himself heard he took it back and read it himself at the top of his voice. It soon became clear that it was a letter from Christie's outlining a secret bidding arrangement that Mr. Simon was to use when bidding for the Rembrandt. It said:

When Mr. Simon is sitting down he is bidding. If he bids openly he is also bidding. When he stands up he has stopped bidding. If he sits down again he is not bidding unless he raises his finger. Having raised his finger he is bidding until he stands up again.

Confronted with the letter, Mr. Chance decided that the bidding must be resumed where it had left off. Mr. Somerset made a mild protest but was overruled. There was only one more bid— the American's 760,000 guineas. As he knocked the picture down for the second time the auctioneer announced in a loud, clear voice, "The Norton Simon Foundation." Mr. Simon's complicated plan to keep his identity secret had failed and, in doing so, had soured Christie's moment of triumph over Sotheby's, from whom they had snatched not only the record for the highest-priced picture but also that for the biggest total turnover at a single sale in Britain, £1,186,279.

Some people blamed Mr. Simon, others thought it was Christie's own fault for accepting such an absurdly involved bidding code.

But for the press the story could scarcely have been better. It had everything—big money, a row, mystery, everything except sex (and some reporters even managed to hint at that by reminding their readers that Lady Cook, who sold the Rembrandt, was the seventh wife of Sir Francis Cook). There was so much to write about that many other interesting aspects of the sale were completely ignored and a much crazier example of secret bidding carried out in the reporters' midst went unreported (except by me).

A few minutes before the Rembrandt came up, one of the directors of Agnew's left his seat in the body of the room, joined the photographers and reporters near the auctioneer's rostrum and began to bid for Lot 101A, a Nativity, only 5¾ by 3¾ inches, by Fra Bartolommeo. To the majority of people in the sale room it must have appeared that he was a very coy fellow consulting his own feet for advice between bids. Only those near him realized that he was relaying bids from a young man who had come into the room by the back door and was now sitting at his feet giving him instructions. At 20,000 guineas the young man gave up and left by the back door, shrouded in an air of mystery and a drab raincoat. The picture was bought in at 22,000 guineas, and the Agnew's man returned to his seat.

The great variety of ways of bidding would make an interesting subject for a student of psychology. Even the way in which a man or woman waves a catalogue is revealing, not only of character but also of circumstance. I once commented to an auctioneer on the way in which a Continental dealer flicked his catalogue in just the same couldn't-care-less fashion whether he was bidding in fivers or five-thousands. "That's because it wasn't his own money," said the auctioneer. "He was working on commission." But no one has ever explained to me why a certain Parisian dealer, a woman, bids by giving the auctioneer a succession of unsubtle winks.

Still a wink is as good as a nod, and, from the auctioneer's point of view, the clearer it is, the better. In spite of this, most regular frequenters of the sale rooms prefer to bid unobtrusively, even furtively, for the spirit of Joseph Duveen (who would often out-bid his rivals on principle, whether he wanted a picture or not) is not completely dead. Auctioneers flourish on the rivalry of the dealers, and it is therefore to a dealer's advantage if he can keep his intentions to himself. Sometimes he will go to great lengths to achieve this. He may, for example, bid up to a certain point and then make a show of dropping out, whereas in fact the clerk or someone unknown to his rivals has taken over from him. The mere fact that a leading dealer—an Agnew, a Colnaghi, a Knoedler or a Wildenstein perhaps—is seen to be bidding for a particular picture is often equivalent to publishing a free valuation of the picture, and in these days, when more and more private collectors are buying direct from the sale rooms, this can mean a serious loss to a dealer. A collector does not have to be very clever to work out that, dealers' profit ratios being what they are, he will probably get a picture he wants much cheaper by outbidding a dealer at an auction than he will ever be able to get it at a later date. This procedure is not, however, recommended to beginners, for, as I have shown elsewhere, it can be very hazardous. It is certainly not for you yet, so let us go back to your sale, which is now getting toward its end.

All the most important lots have gone, many of the prices have run into four figures, one or two have made over £10,000, and the fact that your picture is in such a good sale seems to augur well. You are perhaps a little worried that many people, including some of the dealers, have already left, but your common sense tells you that the number of prospective buyers for any particular picture must always be very few. You need only two keen would-be buyers. Even if there is only one you may get your reserve price or a little more than that. You keep your fingers crossed as the auc-tioneer says, "Lot So-and-so. Fifty pounds, anybody?" Only fifty

pounds? What is he doing, trying to give it away? "Fifty pounds?"
You feel panicky. Doesn't anybody want it even at fifty pounds?
You feel desperate enough to start the bidding yourself. But then
the auctioneer, whose impassivity you had previously admired
but now find maddening, says, "Fifty pounds I'm bid." He pauses
for a moment. "Eighty. . . . One hundred. . . . One twenty.
. . . One fifty. . . . One eighty." Another pause. He repeats,
"One eighty," and looks round the room. "Two hundred. . . .
And fifty." (A bigger jump there, but no one seems to notice.)
". . . Three hundred." Again he searches the room. Just one more
bid at this rate and he has reached your reserve. By now that is
all you are hoping for. The idea of getting the picture back unsold
after all this is unbearable.

"Are you bidding, madam?" says the auctioneer to a woman in
the tenth row. Oh no, she says. She was only shading her eyes
with her catalogue! Please let *someone* bid, you say to yourself.
And the auctioneer says, "Three hundred and fifty." You are
home! But are you? You cannot be sure it is not a Finkelbaum or
Hogginbotham bid. No, it can't be, you tell yourself, or surely the
auctioneer would not have waited so long before making it. "Four
hundred. . . . Four hundred pounds, then . . ." Relief is followed immediately by wild hopes. Perhaps it will go much higher.
A thousand, even? "Four hundred pounds," says the auctioneer,
and you see him raise the little ivory hammer head in his left
hand. But just as he raps it down one of the dealers in the front
row says, "Four twenty." Quickly the auctioneer retrieves the situation. "With the hammer," he says. "I'm sorry. It's four hundred
and twenty pounds, against you, sir." The bidder who thought
he had been successful at £400 comes back equally quickly with
another bid. "Four hundred and fifty," says the auctioneer to the
front-row dealer, who shakes his head. And that is it. The auctioneer repeats, "Four hundred and fifty," taps his hammer and

says a name. You didn't catch the name. But you can be sure it wasn't Finkelbaum or Hogginbotham.

The rest of the sale holds no interest for you. You are wondering whether it was all worth the strain. The price is exactly as they said, between four and five hundred. When they have deducted their ten per cent commission (it would have been much more in any other country) and a small charge for insurance, you will get a little less than £405. Now you begin to think that if only you could have taken it direct to the dealer who bought it, or even to that one in the front row, you would have got more. But don't you believe it. The rivalry of the sale room usually obliges the dealer to pay a higher price there than he would to a private vendor, especially an inexperienced private vendor. Be content. You did very well for a beginner. And if one day when you are in St. James's you see what appears to be a newly painted version of your picture in a dealer's window, don't be surprised (it is amazing what cleaning can do). Go in and ask how much it is. Then try to keep your temper. One hundred per cent profit is nothing in the art game.

10

Dealers, Geese and Golden Eggs

Formerly there was a real need for art. Today the art dealers create a pseudo demand, sitting like vultures on the dead body of art.
—P. K. HOENICH,
Robot Art,
quoted in *Ark*, No. 35 (1964)

Inevitably one had to start thinking of oneself more as a capital broker than as the purveyor of luxury goods one used to be in the past.
—GEOFFREY AGNEW,
London art dealer

The fact that you sold your flower piece in the sale room is significant. Ten years ago you would almost certainly have taken it to a dealer. The current fashion among private individuals to sell at auction is an even bigger thorn in the sides of the dealers than the growing habit of collectors to buy for themselves in the sale rooms. It hurts their pride. Their roles as the kings of the business have been largely usurped by the auctioneers, upon whom they are now much more dependent than ever before. In the old days a nobleman who wished to raise a few thousand pounds on the family heirlooms, for example, would almost invariably have ap-

147

proached one of the great dealers in confidence. Today he not only goes to Sotheby's or Christie's but also permits his name to be published in the sale catalogue and hence in the press. The old, gentlemanly deal, in which the seller was satisfied with a reasonable price that made it possible for the dealer to sell at a reasonable price and so make another of his clients happy, is replaced by a cutthroat duel in the sale room. The effects of this are reflected in two remarks made by one of the directors of Agnew's.* "My family has lived for one hundred and fifty years largely by selling pictures to one generation and buying them back from the next," he said. And then, a few sentences later: "The trouble today is not to sell the finest pictures but to find them in the first place."

But although the private owner of Old Masters who sells at auction has created a big headache for the big dealers (the smaller dealers probably prefer the free-for-all), the private buyer of Old Masters in the sale room is too rare a bird to cause him much trouble. Very few of the wealthy collectors of Old Masters who might seriously menace the big dealers in the sale room have the knowledge to do so. They can, if they wish, make use of the advice of the auctioneers' experts, but they do so at their own risk. Whereas a reputable dealer will give a guarantee of authenticity, the auctioneers disclaim all responsibility for "errors of description, or for the genuineness or authenticity of any lot." So the collector who is spending thousands of pounds on an Old Master still wisely prefers to spend a few more thousands for the benefit of the dealer's expert knowledge and the obligation that his reputation imposes upon him to guarantee what he sells.

When we come to Impressionist and modern pictures, however, things are very different, because the problem of authentication is not nearly so great. During the past few years private buyers in

---

* Quoted by John Pearson in the London *Sunday Times Colour Supplement*, March 17, 1963.

the sale room have spoiled the Impressionist market from the dealer's point of view by forcing the prices so high that there is much less margin left for the dealer's profit. In 1964 the position was made even better for the private buyer (and, therefore, worse for the dealer) when Sotheby's introduced a new condition, relating only to "Impressionist and Modern" sales, which gave them the authority to rescind the sale of any lot of which it was shown, within three weeks, that there was "serious doubt as to authenticity." But we need shed no tears over the dealers. The general increase of business in their trade more than compensates for any pirate raids the collector may make on what was once almost exclusively their territory. You have only to count up the number of prosperous commercial galleries in London to see that business is booming as never before.

Today there are well over a hundred commercial art galleries in London, the great majority of them within the square mile bounded by Oxford Street, Regent Street, Park Lane and King Street, St. James's. Some have been there a hundred years or more; one at least is likely to have opened only last month. For various reasons dealers in most trades have always tended to congregate in a particular district. And the reason for this concentration is obvious. Art is expensive, and this is where the money is. Though Mayfair is no longer predominantly a residential area for the rich it is still the place where they spend their money, just as it was ninety years ago when Agnew's moved into their converted coachhouse in Bond Street, just as it was in 1843 when Christie's opened their doors in King Street. Although in recent times a number of galleries have been successfully established outside this area, it remains the heart of the art market. But inside this heart revolutionary changes have taken place since the war.

Until then, in spite of the swashbuckling activities of Duveen, the trade went on in much the same quiet way as it had for a century or two, following the pattern set by the demand of more or less serious art collectors for a supply of more or less important Old Masters. But after the last war, as inflation created large numbers of collectors whose primary interest in art was its relative safety as an investment, two major changes developed. First, as the run on good Old Masters revealed that supplies were getting very low and that it was not enough simply to charge the earth for those that remained, new supplies—or, rather, supplies of something new—had to be found. The Impressionists and the Post-Impressionists were the obvious answer, and after them the masters of the École de Paris and even a few British homegrown artists. The second change (it may have been first, the two were related chicken–eggwise) came about when the possibilities of the art trade began to attract the attention of certain gentlemen whose knowledge of art may have been limited but who, perhaps because of this, perceived that there was no reason why it should not be marketed by the same modern, high-pressure sales methods that were proving so successful in less hallowed fields of commerce.

The effect on the old-style dealers was at first traumatic, but for most it turned out later to be therapeutic, a shock treatment from which they emerged with renewed vigor to battle with the newcomers. A few of the older Old Master dealers made token protests at being turned into investment brokers, but soon allowed their wounded pride to be assuaged by the increased profits that accrued. For every one of the old brigade who succumbed there were half a dozen newcomers to take his place, most of them fired by the prospect of fat profits made all the more attractive for having been wrung from "culture." Among the scores of men and women who have begun art dealing and/or have opened galleries in London in the years since the war are a typewriter salesman, a zip-fastener wholesaler, a chemist, a cotton manufacturer, a launderette proprietor, a framer, an archaeologist, a professional Quaker, the heir to a cooking-fats fortune, a City financier's son, an ex–colonel of the guards, several Old Etonians, an economist, and a dozen refugees from Europe. By no means everyone who attempted to break in stayed in. Many learned the hard way that there is much more to successful art dealing than opening up shop in Bond Street or its environs and waiting for rich Americans from Claridge's or the Westbury to drop in and buy. But for some there was spectacular success, none more spectacular than that of Frank Lloyd and Harry Fischer, two Austrian refugees whose impact on the art trade has been felt far beyond Bond Street, in Europe and America.

Although both from Vienna, where Fischer was a bookseller and Lloyd owned a string of petrol service stations, they met for the first time during the war while serving in that curious cosmopolitan section of the British Army, the Pioneer Corps. The story goes that while still in khaki they agreed that after the war they would, in partnership, make themselves the biggest art merchants in Europe. Whether the story is true or not is now a purely academic question. The fact is that Marlborough Fine Art, the firm they started in Bond Street in 1946, is not merely the biggest business in the European art league, it is the biggest in the world league.

It is unlikely that the success of Marlborough Fine Art could be repeated again in our time unless (and God forbid that it should happen) the inflationary circumstances that made it possible were repeated. But there are still plenty of opportunities for the enterprising to make a pile, or at any rate a living, the art way. It is not necessary to have a gallery in the West End of London. It is not necessary to have a gallery anywhere. One of London's richest dealers has only a small office and a store room. Others work successfully without leaving their homes except to go to sales. Several dealers sell almost entirely by post, several more ship everything they buy direct to the United States.

To be a dealer, then, all one has to do is to know where and what to buy and where and for how much it can be sold. This may mean, as it does for one dealer I know, an elaborate card index of scores of sources of supply and thousands of customers, each of whom has a special interest—one wants topographical drawings of the county he was born in, another collects paintings by artists whose names begin with Z, a third wants prints of anything to do with railways, and so on. To another dealer, who knows from long experience the sort of quality in pictures that the big auctioneers will accept for sale, it simply means buying works of that quality at the smaller auction houses and taking them along to Sotheby's or Christie's, where almost invariably they will fetch appreciably more than he has paid for them. To a third, who may know very little about painting but who works on the reasonable assumption that virtually everything sold at Sotheby's or Christie's must have some value, it means attending every picture sale in those places, being ready to snap up anything that is going for a few pounds and, later, selling it to other dealers or putting it back in the sale room again. His motto is "There is at least one bargain in every sale." And he is right.

The process of "selling pictures to one generation and buying them back from the next" by which Agnew's achieved prosperity has a parallel today. As any regular frequenter of the auction rooms and art galleries can see, the same sort of thing is happening all the time on a lower level and at a speeded-up rate. A certain proportion of pictures at any one time is circulating like a chain letter among dealers, private buyer-speculators and sale rooms. In most cases everyone concerned makes a profit, but one cannot help feeling that, as with chain letters, there is a catch somewhere. Someone at the end of the line, it seems, must lose. But this is not necessarily true. In recent years art prices generally rose so rapidly and consistently that however much a buyer was "stung" for a work by an artist with a market rating, it was usually only a matter of waiting two or three years before it was possible for him to resell it at a profit—even to the dealer from whom he had bought it in the first place. I remember once upsetting a wealthy collector by remarking tactfully that a Post-Impressionist picture he had just bought from a dealer for £25,000 had been bought by the dealer in the sale room only a few months earlier for £16,000. He was livid. He had no idea the dealers made so much profit. It was criminal, he said, and threatened to tell the dealer what he thought of him, etc. The fact that he had been "cheated" put him off the picture so much that inside two years he put it in the sale room. It fetched £32,000. So far as I am aware he did not then feel that he must share his profit with the dealer. But he does now think the dealer is a wonderful chap and always buys from him.

In this case the dealer's profit, although it may seem very high, was ultimately fully justified. He had bought cheaply, and even after he had added more than fifty per cent profit the price was still reasonable. Generally, if a dealer buys at a bargain price he will fix his selling price accordingly. He will calculate his profit broadly in accordance with a descending scale of percentages that begins at 100 per cent or more on items for which he has paid up to, say, £500, falls to fifty per cent on items that cost him £20,000 and to twenty-five per cent on £50,000. In this way the dealers have established a general price range whose relation to sale-room prices should be understood by the collector-investor who is thinking primarily of a quick profit. Without that knowledge he may find himself in the position of the woman who, having put her £40,000 Impressionist picture into the sale room from which (although she did not know it) the dealer had bought it for £26,000 only two years earlier, was surprised when it failed to fetch as much as she had paid for it.

Understandably, most dealers are reluctant to let their clients know what they themselves have paid for the pictures they sell, but in many cases their secrets are no secrets. A surprisingly large proportion of the pictures sold by London dealers are bought in the principal London sale rooms, each of which issues price lists after every sale. Very often, therefore, the prospective buyer of a picture can discover without much trouble what profit the dealer is making. For the big-time dealer there would seem to be an additional problem in that many of his purchases are reported in the press, but according to several I have talked with this is not so. Press publicity of this sort can be of tremendous value in drawing the attention of prospective buyers, especially public galleries in this country and abroad, to the availability of an important picture. Because of the way in which most great public galleries are controlled, purchasing is generally done by committees. This means that they rarely buy direct from the sale rooms, but must wait until a picture is in the hands of a dealer so that they can borrow it and sit on it in committee until agreement is reached. From the taxpayer's or ratepayer's point of view this is a crazy way of going on, but it suits the dealers very well, especially as dispensers of public money rarely haggle about prices.

In justification of the big profit made on a high-priced picture it should be remembered that often a very risky gamble is involved, that in many cases it may mean that a large capital sum is tied up for a long period before a buyer is found, that during that period the value of the picture at auction will probably have risen automatically by several thousand pounds, and that the business of finding the buyer may itself be costly. When, for example, Claude Lorrain's *A View of Carthage, with Dido, Aeneas and Their Suite Leaving for the Hunt* was bought by the Hamburg Kunsthalle for £70,000 (a large part of it from the city's football-pools levy) from the Hallsborough Gallery in 1964, simple arithmetic pointed to a profit of more than £15,000. But the picture had been bought (at Christie's) nearly two years earlier. The price, £54,600, was then, and still is, an auction record for a picture by Claude, but it is reasonable to assume that during the time it was in the dealer's hands its auction value rose two or three thousand pounds simply by virtue of the general uptrend of the market in pictures of this quality. It also rose many more thousands of pounds by virtue of the tremendous international publicity it received after it was the subject of an extraordinarily successful one-picture exhibition (suggested, and partly organized, by me for a fee of £50). Incidentally, the picture was also reframed by the Hallsborough Gallery at a cost of £600, a figure which may be taken as representative of the boom that has made picture framing more profitable than picture dealing for a handful of top craftsmen.

But, to come down to earth, let me recall the remarkable price histories of a few humbler pictures that I observed going the rounds in recent years. The first concerns one of those very fly characters known as knockers whom we met in Chapter Six—that is, the small-time dealers, usually, as in this case, furniture or antique dealers, who buy their stock by calling at private houses and persuading unsuspecting housewives to part with anything saleable. (A rather more respectable form of knocking is practiced by even the highest-class dealers and auctioneers. Few of them would hesitate to pull strings to get introductions to owners of Old Masters rumored to be hard up and thinking of selling—Joe Duveen was the king of such knockers—and those more interested in modern pictures are not above importuning the widows and families of famous modern artists.) Our particular knocker bought a water color for £2 and sold it to another of his fraternity for £5. This second knocker put it into a minor London sale room, where it was sold for £14. The buyer, a small-time picture dealer, sold it before he had left the sale room to a collector-speculator for £25. This gentleman took it to Sotheby's, where, a few months later, it was bought by a West End dealer for £55. The dealer put it in his annual Christmas-present show at £120 and sold it to a collector who, so far as I am aware, still has it. The water color is by Edward Lear, whose prices have risen so much since this happened—in 1963—that the collector could now get his money back by selling at Sotheby's or Christie's.

I was in at the beginning of my second history, which began in late 1964 and is still progressing. I walked into a minor London sale room just as what appeared, at ten yards' distance, to be a very attractive little landscape was being knocked down at £14. Having boobed once or twice in the past by buying attractive-looking pictures that I had not examined in advance, I resisted the temptation to bid, but after the sale I asked the buyer, a suburban dealer, if I might see it. The little picture had been catalogued as "Ibbetson" and we both agreed that it could be by that artist.* I offered to buy it on the spot at four times the price he had paid, but the dealer wanted to "do some work on it first." This work, I learned subsequently, consisted primarily in taking the picture to one of the biggest Old Master dealers in Bond Street, asking his opinion and offering it for sale. The big man's opinion was that it was not by Ibbetson but that it was worth £70. The little man sold. Imagine his surprise, then, when I told him, a few weeks later, that "his" picture was in the Christmas exhibition of an off–Bond Street dealer (nothing to do with the big man) and priced at £320. And that was not all. In June 1965 I saw the picture in a Knightsbridge antique shop and asked the price. "Four hundred and twenty guineas," replied the antique dealer.

The third history concerns a "runner"—a man who acts as an agent to other dealers, keeping his eyes and ears open for anything that may interest them, while all the time nursing the hope that he will one day be able to set up as a dealer himself. This runner bought an Old Master drawing so cheaply at a country sale that he decided to keep it to himself. He put it into a London sale, where it made £40—nearly eight times as much as

---

* Julius Caesar Ibbetson (1759–1817).

he had paid for it. The buyer, a small-time dealer, sold it to one of the West End dealers whom the runner often helped, for £100. But that was not the end. In the meantime the runner had described the drawing to an American dealer, who was very interested and asked to see it. Without mentioning that it was no longer his the runner promised to bring it to him. He went to the West End dealer, who was now offering the drawing at £400, and said that he thought he could sell it for him. The dealer let him have it and promised him ten per cent commission if he made a sale. The American was very impressed by the drawing and asked how much it was. The runner quickly added another hundred to the price—and got it! It is probably only a matter of time before the drawing comes back to the London sale room to be sold as part of an important American collection of Old Master drawings. Things of this sort are happening all the time. There is probably some such story behind a large proportion of all the pictures, especially the older ones, that come onto the market. But not all of them are quite so happy for all concerned. There is the sad tale of the young art reporter who, when hard up, sold to a friend for £20 a gouache given to him by an artist whose work he had praised (see reference to critics' "perks" in the next chapter). When the artist suddenly became successful the young man cunningly bought back the gouache for £25 and sold it to a dealer for £80. The dealer hung it in his gallery, priced at £150. The reporter was very angry at having been "done." A little later he was even angrier when he saw a similar gouache in another gallery, marked "£320" on the back. Then he had the bright idea of buying back his gouache from the first dealer, who generously let him have it for £120, and offering it to the second dealer for £220. But the second dealer laughed and showed him his own gouache, which, he said, he would gladly sell for £90. The "£320" on the back, he explained, was the price of the picture that had been in the frame before the gouache. Exit young art reporter, crestfallen.

In my experience it is usually the get-rich-quick, fly-by-night, small-time dealers who try to make exorbitant profits that have no fair relation to a picture's present or potential value. The wise dealer (and most of the well-established ones are very wise) knows just how far he can go without frightening a client away. Those dealers who run galleries in which they show the work of living artists will explain that much of the money they make on *dealing* goes to subsidize exhibitions of work by new artists. Although this may be little consolation to the man who pays £40,000 for a £30,000 picture, there is in most cases a measure of truth in the explanation. Few dealers in the West End of London could survive on the proceeds of the one-man shows by living artists that they hold. Many regard them simply as window dressing. The really profitable business is done behind the scenes usually by selling the work of dead artists. Until Marlborough Fine Art's high-powered promotion of artists like Sutherland, Bacon, Ben Nicholson, and Ceri Richards showed the way to make British art pay, most dealers had no alternative but to regard exhibitions of work by British artists as acts of altruism. But because Marlborough have made a handful of British artists pay in a big way this does not mean that the whole picture has changed. The number of serious British artists (that is, artists who should be taken seriously) whose one-man shows are financially worth while for the dealer cannot be more than a few dozen. Those outside the Marlborough stable who make big money can be numbered on your thumbs.

Generally, when an artist has a one-man show the dealer's share is 33⅓ per cent of the proceeds of all sales. In some cases it is as high as 50 per cent. The considerable cost of framing has to be met by the artist, but the dealer usually pays for the catalogues

and may provide an opening-night party. When he gives an unknown artist an exhibition the dealer takes a gamble that justifies
the high rate of commission. But there is no reduction in the rate
of commission if the artist proves to be a big success. The 33⅓
per cent will continue to be exacted from his sales at all subsequent exhibitions. Thus the dealer's initial gamble can prove to
be usefully profitable and he may decide it is to his advantage
to bind the artist to him by a contract, on the principle that, as
one dealer put it, it is silly to buy golden eggs when you can buy
the goose that lays them.

Such contracts may carry with them an agreement by which
the dealer pays a regular monthly "salary" to the artist which is
offset against his sales. Although arrangements of this sort have
existed in France since the beginning of the century, they were
virtually unknown in Britain until after the last war. First to start
giving contracts in London were three dealers who had learned
the trade in Paris, Charles and Peter Gimpel of Gimpel Fils and
Erica Brausen of the Hanover Gallery. But it was not until about
1960, when Marlborough Fine Art moved into the field, that the
practice began to become fairly widespread.

At that time Marlborough's highly successful activities were
causing some envy and ill feeling among older established dealers. It was particularly galling for those who, after having nursed
certain British artists to the point where they were beginning to
yield handsome returns, found that those artists were succumbing
to the lure of contracts from Marlborough that would provide
them with handsome and regular incomes, relieve them of such
mundane worries as income tax problems and guarantee them
exhibitions in London's most up-to-date gallery. But there was
also a sneaking admiration for Marlborough's enterprise, and this
showed itself in ways that were all to some extent beneficial to the
artists. Many dealers began to spruce up their galleries and give
them a new look and new lighting. Ideas among the dealers about

the monetary value of contemporary British art changed—to the advantage of the artists and the dealers and, in the long run, of the collectors. Following Marlborough's example, too, those dealers who were agents for British artists showed increased support for their artists in the sale rooms, bidding for any of their works that came up for auction to ensure that their prices were maintained. In nearly all the activities of dealers in modern paintings Marlborough set the pace and continues to do so. Some ill feeling toward them still exists, but the phrase "doing a Marlborough," originally coined as a term of opprobrium, now has another connotation that implies a grudging admiration.

Most criticism of the contract system is based on the romantic, *vie de Bohème* fallacy that artists do their best work when they are starving and that comfort and security are inimical to inspiration. But it is also said that the system gives the dealer too much power over the artist, that the artist is no longer his own master and is told not only when, where and for how much his work shall be sold but also what sort of pictures he must paint, and in this there is certainly some truth. In the old days an artist had a one-man show when he had enough good work ready. Now, if he is a "tied" artist, he is likely to be working always with an exhibition date hanging over him. And he is likely to be working with the primary object of selling rather than creating. If, in doing this, he is inclined to play safe and repeat the sort of things with which he has been successful in the past, he may well be encouraged to do so by his dealer.

Whether a contract is a good thing depends very much on the temperament of the artist. Some artists find no difficulty at all in fulfilling themselves and the terms of the contract. Others are temperamentally unsuited to working to deadlines and are unable to say no to anything their dealers suggest. I have known one of Britain's most distinguished painters so pressed for time that he had to paint half the pictures for his biennial one-man show in a month (and that was how the exhibition looked). And I have seen what looked suspiciously like potboiler drawings served up, to meet a demand, by one of our greatest sculptors.

But in spite of its dangers (and in the case of the young artist prematurely signed up and pressure-promoted by a high-powered dealer they can be very great) I think that the contract system has done more good than harm, and I would like to see it spread. It is obvious, however, that it must always be limited to a very small proportion of working artists, for no dealer will give a contract to an artist unless he is fairly sure that he will pay his way, and the number of artists that even today's booming art market can or will support to the tune of even £100 per month is comparatively few.

I have said that to be a dealer all one has to know is where and what to buy and where and for how much to sell it, but if I make it sound easy that is a mistake, a mistake that many would-be dealers have made. As I have shown again and again, the field is vast and is thick with booby traps. For this reason most dealers specialize in a particular part of the field and may know surprisingly little about the other parts. A few years ago the writer Clement Freud decided to test whether London's top art dealers were frank, helpful, knowledgeable. Writing of his experiences, in *The Queen* magazine, he came to the conclusion that "the answers loosely would appear to be yes, yes, no." His test consisted of hawking three nondescript little pictures and a "£4,000" Renoir drawing signed "AR" round a number of galleries and asking for any offers. He wore a day's growth of beard and gave a false name. At Spink's, a firm that specializes in antiquities and coins, the Renoir was, understandably perhaps, not even recognized as a Renoir. The same thing happened at Wildenstein's, where, if the bosses were at lunch, even the office boy might reasonably have been expected to know a Renoir. Agnew's, who are primarily Old Master men, thought it was most likely by Renoir but were not interested enough to make an offer. At Marlborough Fine Art two young men argued about it, one rejecting the idea that it was by Renoir, the other suggesting it might be a Renoir forgery. Only Tooth's representative thought it might be worth a lot of money* and advised taking it to a Renoir expert for authentication.

As a test of dealers' knowledge it was hardly fair, since it would appear that only at Spink's and Tooth's was the opinion given by a senior member of the firm. It might equally well have been said to illustrate the honesty of dealers, not only because they gave their opinions so frankly, but because even where the Renoir was recognized no attempt was made to take advantage of Freud's feigned anxiety to raise money on it. One aspect of the account that might justly have caused some concern, however, was that all the dealers appear to have accepted without suspicion Freud's story that he had found the pictures in the attic of a house he had just bought. Yet the Renoir had been shown at the O'Hana Gallery a few years before and had been bought there by a well-known collector (who had lent it to Freud for his experiment). So much for the oft-quoted theory that such works are so well recorded that it would be impossible for a thief to sell them. (We shall return to that in Chapter Twelve.)

The really successful dealer is a man who combines something of the psychologist, the stockbroker, the impresario, the public-relations man and the detective, with a touch of aesthetic sensibility and some knowledge of artists' methods of working. He has insight into the collector's mentality; the ability to anticipate price trends and the power to create them; a sense of showmanship in presenting his wares and an understanding of the value of publicity; a nose for what is good and for what is false; enough knowledge of techniques to be one jump ahead of most of his clients and to talk intelligently to the others; and such enthusiasm

---

* In April 1964 the drawing came up for sale at Sotheby's—and was knocked down at £1,800!

for what he is selling, whether it is by an Old Master, a very minor Impressionist or the latest young unknown in his stable, that his clients feel he is doing them a favor. An instinctive flair for the game and the experience that comes from years of handling pictures will be far more valuable to him than any amount of book learning. Duveen, who, in Behrman's words, "seldom read anything," was interested in art books only when they confirmed his own opinions. When he was asked, in the course of one of his many lawsuits, if he knew Ruskin's *Stones of Venice* he replied that he "had heard of the picture but never actually seen it." And when his *gaffe* was pointed out to him afterward he just laughed. He could afford to. When he died, in 1939, he left the best part of a million pounds.

11

Critics, et Cetera

The ultimate critic of all art is time.
—PILLOO R. POCHKANAWALA,
Indian artist, quoted in
The Illustrated Weekly of India,
Sept. 22, 1963

Read everything that you can find about art except the reviews.
—BEN SHAHN,
The Shape of Content

Those critics! There's a lot of double-talk going on. They've invented words.
—JOE HIRSHHORN,
American collector, in an
interview in *Art Voices,* Nov. 1962

Politicians disgust me. Art critics also; they're just jugglers, dodgers.
—SCOTTIE WILSON,
British "primitive" artist,
quoted in *The Studio,* June 1962

A man has to have a gizzard like an ostrich to digest all the brass tacks and wire nails of modern art theories.
—D. H. LAWRENCE,
from "Making Pictures,"
The Studio, July 1929

The more we learn, the more there is to learn. This simple paradox is as old as man himself, but never before has its universality been so evident as it is today. The concept of the expanding universe is seen to apply not only in the field of astrophysics but in every sphere of man's pursuit of knowledge. The further he pushes out toward its frontiers, the more those frontiers recede. This law applies as much to the arts as it does to the sciences. It has always applied to them and will always apply to them. And if they are to be understood, it must be understood. Art criticism, then, must start from this concept, and from the knowledge that true art is not a self-contained department of life but an integral part that influences and is influenced by all its other parts. Today, when, as we shall see in a later chapter, art and science seem to be heading for marriage, we are inclined to forget that they have been consorting together for thousands of years. Knowledge made available by science has always influenced the artist's vision, and since the Stone Age he has depended on science for his materials. Scientific knowledge of biology and anatomy, of light and of the atmosphere, of psychology and optics, for example, have all had major effects on painting. Today we are seeing the effects of scientific research and discovery not only in the paintings painters are painting but also in the way in which many of them are turning from paint as a medium to the new materials that technology has made available.

What, more than anything else, makes the painting and sculpture of today different from that of any earlier age is the degree of the artist's consciousness of this interrelation of art and science. In a letter dated October 14, 1914, two years before he died, the German painter Franz Marc wrote: "I have not found the adjustment between modern science and art which I had in mind. However, it must be found and not *au détriment des sciences* . . . [Art] will not live in a state of enmity with science."* Then Marc was almost alone in the search. In the past decade legions of artists have been preoccupied with it. This put a burden on the art critic that he has so far shown himself incapable of bearing.

* Quoted in *Modern German Art,* by "Peter Thoene."

166

Generally unable himself to grasp what is happening, and unable
to differentiate between the genuine and the phony aspects of the
movement, he has evaded his responsibility—defined by Picasso
as "building a bridge people can walk over to join the artist"—
and has built a great wall of jargon round himself and around art
to keep the layman out. By making himself unreadable he hopes,
presumably, to make himself impregnable. And so, in a sense, he
is. For inside the wall everyone is playing the emperor's-new-
clothes game and outside there is apathy or the sort of pity usually
felt for lunatics. With a few notable exceptions art critics nowadays seem to be writing exclusively for other inmates of their own
precious little asylum.

How did this come about? In 1961 the American critic Dore
Ashton made out a case to show that "the language of art evaluation has been debased . . . primarily by the notion of *utility* in
art." She cited the example of a dealer who interrupted her pleas-
urable admiration of a piece of sculpture by explaining, "This
artist is interested in the plastic mobility of the sculptural mass."
"I recognized this," Miss Ashton wrote,* "as talk for the client. It
is suitable, scientific-sounding jargon which pretends to give an
explanation of a work of art. Instead of being a beautiful aesthetic
fact, with its own intrinsic meaning, the sculpture becomes a
'problem' similar to the scientist's problem, and seems therefore
to have some possible end other than purely aesthetic. This makes
it all right." Miss Ashton quoted the dealer's idiotic comment
to illustrate the way in which Americans had come to think about
modern art, and she laid the responsibility for this at the doors of
American art schools that overstressed the importance of applied
art and sought to elevate it above the fine arts. But, well argued
though her case was, Miss Ashton could not disguise the fact that
primarily the fault lay not with the art schools but with her col-

---

* In *Arts & Architecture,* October 1961.

leagues and predecessors, the critics who evolved the meaning-less vocabulary of criticism, which since 1961 has continued to proliferate like a cancer.

In Britain, where, after the first big exhibition of the "new American painting" at the Tate Gallery in 1956, the critics, like the painters, fell over themselves in their haste to emulate their American counterparts, the debasement of the "language of art evaluation" was all the more marked for being secondhand. To the layman it appeared that, art itself having gone mad, the critics had decided that the best way to convey to their readers a sense of that madness was to try to match it with written madness of their own. It might perhaps have been claimed for such a decision that it was logical, but the result, at least as the uninitiated saw it, was a torrent of irrational gibberish that made the already con-fusing elements of modern art doubly confusing. At risk of being accused of eating my fellow dogs (and quoting out of context), let me give you a few examples from Britain and the United States of the sort of thing I mean:

In the end they are reabsorbed into the incommensurability and into the indefinite opening of the void of the cycle of external relations which ordain among themselves in the expanse of the surroundings.

Or:

Even in the least colourful of his previous paintings colour had helped to accentuate the formal re-birth of matter, stressing outlines and tracing borders between the centres endowed with a stronger in-tensity of existence and the inarticulate pereikon of the canvas.

Or:

The primary formal nucleus is a fissured ovoid form which incarnates the minimal, specifically sculptural articulation, connotes the promise of birth, the suggestion of death-in-life, of destruction, extinction. The form is, if you like, Brancusi's, re-invented, invested with a pathos created by medium (bronze, plaster, cement), roughness, explication of the dialectic and ambiguity which it prefigures, assimilation into a broad sculptural context. This nucleus of a vocabulary grows, is modified, varied, integrated in an enormous range of modes, into those major works through which a general sculptural syntax is developed.

Often a critic, in his anxiety to display his own erudition or originality, will read into an artist's work esoteric ideas that the artist never had and, probably, was quite incapable of having. The critic may then argue that the ideas were there in the artist's subconscious, and the artist, if he is a simple man (as so many fine artists are) may believe him and even learn to talk about his work in the quasi-scientific terms invented by the critic. Even where, for all you or I know, it is arguable that the critic is right in his diagnosis—as when that clever word-spinner Pierre Rouve writes of Mario Sironi:

Sironi has illustrated Bergson. This is his greatness which is still to be discovered: the supreme synthesis of his mature works. They are unions of uniques united in unity. Such Heideggerian lilt is not misplaced: alone in Milan, harrowed by the horrors of war, Sironi has painted the most enigmatic thought of Heraclitus in which metaphysic becomes mathematics: "One = All"*

—the question remains: Whom does this sort of criticism help?

Paradoxically, the simpler and emptier the work to be described, the more involved the language became. The impossibility for even the best-intentioned critics to find anything new to say about successive exhibitions of banal hard-edge abstractions and abstract-expressionist paintings, produced by British artists under the influence of the Tate Gallery's American show in 1956,

---

* Rouve, a London art critic, in his introduction to the catalogue of the Sironi exhibition at the Grosvenor Gallery, London, January 1964.

made one suspect that certain critics in the art reviews had a standard form of notice which they re-jigged to suit different artists. Everyone was writing about "space" as if he had created it. *Let there be space,* the critics said, and there was space—thousands of huge, idiotic canvases full of it. Even the artists became convinced that their empty pictures were filled with some exciting new quality called space. No one ever explained coherently what the term meant. It was not the illusion of aerial space created by the use of perspective and tone values. That, one gathered, was out of date and beneath contempt. It had something to do with the way in which a painting directed the spectator's attention away from itself and to the space around it. One way of doing this was by leaving the canvas completely blank except for a few strokes of paint placed as if they were about to fall off the edge of the canvas. Artist Roger Hilton, a pioneer of this genre and one of its leading British exponents, explained his own ideas thus:

I have moved away from the sort of so-called non-figurative painting where lines and colours are flying about in an illusory space; from pictures which still had depth, or from pictures which had space in them; from spatial pictures, in short, to space-creating pictures. The effect is to be felt outside rather than inside the picture: the picture is to be not primarily an image, but a space-creating mechanism . . . a kind of catalyst for the activisation of the surrounding space.*

Ultimately this quest for a sort of painting that would direct the viewer's attention away from itself was crowned with complete success, when thousands of "space" paintings to which no one paid any attention were produced. This was surely the nadir of British painting. The only encouraging thing about it was that anything which followed it *must* be better. (More recently the password has been not "space" but "ambiguity." The facts that

---

*Quoted in Lawrence Alloway, *Nine Abstract Artists.*

light and dark surfaces in an abstract pattern may be read inter-
changeably—i.e., that either may, at the will of the viewer, be
seen to "recede" or to "project"—and that certain painted or
carved images may be read in more than one way, were known to
primitive man. But they were discovered by many artists and by
most art critics only in the 1960s. Thereafter ambiguity, not only
of form but of content, meaning, idea, even of intention, became
the great virtue and was pursued with such schizophrenic inten-
sity that by 1965 an exhibition of British art sent to America
with the blessing of the British Council was officially described
as emphasizing "the growing accent on rich ambiguity" to be seen
in the painting and sculpture of this country.)

It is ironical that in our time, when so many artists, the socialist-
realists or kitchen-sinkers, the Pop boys, the New Realists and the
kinetics fanatics, have talked so much of creating art that is part
of every man's everyday life, the ordinary man finds art becoming more remote than ever from him. The Stone Age artist was,
if we are to believe the anthropologists, striving to invoke magic
by making a naturalistic image. Such critics as he had, therefore,
were likely to be demanding more and more naturalism. And
more than twenty thousand years later, in spite of the millions
and millions of words that have been written in an attempt to
change their minds, the vast majority of twentieth-century men
and women, although unaware of any magic in art, use the same
critical criterion. This is underlined by the fact that the art "education" of the masses, having caught up with Impressionism,
stopped there, because, as Roger Fry pointed out as long ago as
1917, Impressionism "marked the climax of a movement which
had been going on more or less steadily from the thirteenth century—the tendency to approximate the forms of art more exactly
to the representation of the totality of appearance."*

But even Impressionism was popularly accepted only after it

---

* Roger Fry, *Vision and Design.*

had first been debased. In Britain, for instance, the work of such pseudo Impressionists as S. J. Lamorna Birch and W. G. de Glehn were admired before Monet, Pissarro and Sisley. Even today there are millions of people who accept the rubbish perpetrated by contemporary hack artists who call themselves Impressionists much more readily than they accept the masterpieces (particularly the later masterpieces which adumbrated abstraction) of Monet. These are the people who think Picasso is a fraud and all modern art is mad, but who live in homes crowded with Cubist-inspired abstract patterns on wallpapers, curtains, carpets, chair covers, tiles and so on. They would probably argue that wallpaper, dress materials, posters, carpets and other fabrics are the right vehicles for abstract art. And they may be right. In any case, even a debased art that permeates their lives in this way is better than no art at all. It may even be that such people, with their easy and unquestioning acceptance of the mass-produced art that is thrust upon them, are better suited than the more sophisticated of us to inherit the promised wonderful world of the future, the New Babylon,* in which, freed from all work by the machines, man will pass his life in an environment of art that surrounds him like the air and is taken equally for granted. In which, we are told, life itself will be the ultimate and supreme work of art.

But will a man whose life is a work of art need to understand what a work of art is? Is our idea that ultimately everyone should be educated in "appreciation of art" valid? Should we not accept as an axiom based on the experience of the past hundred years that the general public (led in Britain by the Royal Academy) will always lag fifty years behind the most vital art of its own time? Or, to put it in the more usual, euphemistic way, is not the avant-garde artist by definition one who is fifty years ahead of his time? And might we not as well resign ourselves to the fact that in our time the public's attitude to the artist who explores new ideas

---

* See p. 208.

172

THE ART GAME

will always be (as an American critic has put it): "I don't dig what you are doing, therefore you are goofing on the job"?

It seems to me that those of us who have a vested interest in it may well attach too much importance to art or, at any rate, to *understanding* art. Art can be enjoyed without being understood. Indeed, understanding and enjoyment of art might be mutually exclusive. Certainly with understanding of the processes of art comes a change in the quality of enjoyment, and the new "understanding enjoyment" is not necessarily better than the old, spontaneous "ignorant enjoyment." I am inclined to believe that if a poll were taken of children and students who have taken art-appreciation courses in schools and colleges, it would be found that in the majority of cases aesthetic sensibility had been blunted rather than heightened by "taking a Cézanne to pieces" to see how the artist did it or analyzing the sources of inspiration of a Byzantine mosaicist.

Picasso, when asked the meaning of one of his paintings, replied, "What is the meaning of a flower?" And in the same way that a botanist may find that his knowledge of and interest in the structure of a flower supersedes his emotional response to it, so the man who is given an "explanation" of a work of art may find that he has been robbed of his awareness of that work as (to requote Dore Ashton) "a beautiful aesthetic fact, with its own intrinsic meaning." So the critic, especially the one who writes for or speaks to a mass audience, has a tremendous responsibility, an enormous power to do good or harm. That he is failing in his responsibility is not, perhaps, immediately apparent. Public art galleries and the commercial ones, too, report bigger and bigger attendances, and the number of people who can call themselves collectors continues to increase. But unless we believe that it does not matter what motive people have for collecting or what force impels them to visit galleries so long as they do collect and do visit galleries, then we should not feel smug about the statistics.

We know well that the commonest reason why people collect today has little to do with aesthetics, and we would be hard put to
it to prove that increased gallery attendances are much more than
the fruits of a great publicity campaign aimed at "selling" art as
if it were some fashionable new wonder drug. Most of the "critics"
(I quote the term to denote that it includes all those who review
art exhibitions, whether qualified to do so or not) are no more
than nuts in that vast publicity machine upon which Sir Herbert
Read (the best of the British critics) has said the artist is "miser-
ably dependent" and which is his "deepest humiliation."

There are more critics than ever before, but criticism is at its
lowest ebb. Every crazy manifestation of pseudo-avant-garde art
is treated with deadpan seriousness, so that anyone who persists
in wading through the pseudo-intellectual porridge of the art
periodicals (especially the American ones) is given the impression
that great masters are sprouting every week in the commercial
galleries of London, New York, Paris and lesser cities. Never—
well, hardly ever—does a single critic go out on a limb and say
NO. Committed, through fear of repeating the mistakes of those
critics who mauled Manet, castigated Cézanne, reviled Renoir and
pooh-poohed Picasso (and, too often, through fear of offending
an art magazine's dealer advertisers) to a policy of praising everything they see, these critics fail in their first duty—to expose the
false and the phony, to separate the sheep from the greats whom
they (the sheep) follow uncomprehendingly.

Art criticism is becoming as much a free-for-all as art itself.
Soon almost anyone will be able to join in. In Britain the bright
boy just down from university where he has mugged up a little
art history or the failed artist with or without a chip on his shoul-
der, the young would-be poet who finds poetry doesn't pay or the
disillusioned journalist with aesthetic pretensions, need only learn
the current jargon from the art periodicals and he will have little
difficulty in persuading the editor of some sham-intellectual pub-

lication to grant him a space in which to practice the art of writing about art without saying anything comprehensible to anyone but himself. He may or may not be paid for these early exercises; that is probably not important. What is important is that he will now be able to call himself an art critic and enjoy the prestige and the "perks" that go with that position. He will find doors that were previously firmly locked against him swinging open as if by a "magic eye." Artists, even distinguished ones who have no need of the scrap of publicity he can give them, will receive him courteously, talk with him about their work as if he knew what they are talking about and perhaps give him a drawing or let him buy a painting or sculpture at a bargain price. Dealers will welcome him to their galleries almost as warmly as if he were a client and praise what he writes even though they know it is pretentious twaddle. They may even pay him to write some of his pretentious twaddle for the catalogues of their exhibitions. If he is the drinking sort he will be able to drink his fill almost every evening (and some mornings) of every month at parties given to launch the new shows. At these parties he will meet scores of people who think he can be useful to them and some who can be useful to him. He will talk in a loud, clear, authoritative voice and get himself invited to arrange an exhibition for some prestige-giving organization, or to judge a competition for some fee-paying, prestige-seeking industrial concern. And if he plays his cards well he will soon be able to desert the publication that gave him his start, and write for one that pays more in both cash and prestige. Then, from that vantage point, he will, with a little bit of luck, be able to insinuate himself into the critics' Olympus, that Sunday-morning program of the British Broadcasting Corporation in which he and four or five other self-esteemed pundits will pee lukewarm praise or insipid censure from their lofty height onto the achievements of their betters.

But surely, you will be saying, there must be some good critics.

And so there are, but it would be difficult to find more than a handful who do their job with distinction. The majority of "critics," people who, like me, report on and make a few critical comments on art exhibitions for popular newspapers and magazines, would have to be dismissed on the grounds that they are only quasi critics. Another great number would be rejected because they are concerned not at all with building Picasso's bridges but solely with building up their own images and egos. A third ineligible group (which would of course include many from each of the first two groups) would be those who are the main butt of my attack, the jargon writers, the unintelligibles, wizards with words. To qualify as a good critic a writer must first be a man of imagination himself, for, to paraphrase Schiller, there is only one vessel by which a work of imagination can be apprehended and its quality can be transmitted, and that is imagination itself. Diderot, the first to practice art criticism as we know it, wrote that it was the first duty of art to touch and to move, and in this sense his critiques were works of art in that they moved his readers to see, or to want to see, the work he was writing about. As long ago as 1846 Baudelaire, in one of his own pieces of art criticism, explained to later critics how this could be done. The critic, he said, should be partial and passionate, he should have knowledge, but, even more important, he must have strong feelings about art and be able to analyze those feelings. He believed (and supported the belief by his own example) that poets make the best critics. The idea has been echoed again and again in the past hundred years and put pithily by Picasso: "Perhaps it would be better if all critics were poets and wrote poetry instead of pedantry." But although contemporary France has a poet or two who finds inspiration in the visual arts and produces poetic criticism, in Britain and America the best that can be mustered are a number of critics who happen to be poetasters and who, so far as one can judge from their reviews, exercise a strict apartheid between their criticism and their poetry.

We must look elsewhere, then, for our critics. Where? Perhaps among the artists themselves. Contrary to the critic-nurtured myth, artists are for the most part extremely articulate about their own and other artists' work. Sometimes they may get on their high horses and say, like Epstein, "I rest silent in my work." But, dismounted, they usually become, again like Epstein, extraordinarily eloquent. Criticism written by a genuine artist invariably conveys a greater sense of enthusiasm for art than that of the nonartist critic. Because he is a man of imagination his writing will be imaginative. Because art is his life, not just a little corner of it, his approach will be down to earth, he will not romanticize or affect emotions that he does not feel. But for the nonartist critic art is something which he looks at, and responds to, from a self-consciously adopted position. He is neither fish nor fowl, neither artist nor honest spectator. He is forced to strike an attitude, to simulate enthusiasm or register disapproval where he feels only indifference. Unlike the artist, he could, let's face it, dispense with art entirely if it were not a means of livelihood. And, let's face it again, art could probably dispense with him.

In fact, it is possible to foresee the time when even the good critic no longer has any function. The need for him will continue only so long as the gap between artists and the great mass of nonartists exists. His purpose is to close that gap and so hasten his own end. But even if he persists in preaching to the converted in a language the unconverted do not understand, the gap will still be closed and his end will still come. It will come not because every man has been taught to "understand" art, but because art has become so much a part of his everyday environment that he does not demand explanations for it.

12

The Artnappers

> *Your criminals are still on bank robberies and coshing people, they haven't really moved in on the Crime of Civilization.*
> —JOE CHAPMAN,
> New York "museum security consultant," quoted in the *Observer*, Sept. 1964

In July 1961 an article of mine headed "He Walked Out with the Mona Lisa" appeared in the London *Evening News*. It was not, as you might imagine, an article about Mona Lisa's boy friend but a somewhat lurid account of the theft of Leonardo's masterpiece from the Louvre fifty years earlier. It told the story of how a cleaner at the great museum had tucked the picture under his overall one morning and walked out of a back door to the Seine quay, and also an even more incredible story of what happened to the picture during the two years before it was recovered.

The cleaner, an Italian named Vicenzo Perugia, was arrested

when he tried to sell it to a dealer in Florence. In his defense he pleaded that he had only wanted to return the picture to Italy for patriotic reasons; nevertheless, he was sentenced to seven months' imprisonment. The painting was restored to the Louvre shortly before Christmas 1913, but at irregular intervals ever since rumors have circulated that the Louvre picture is a copy. According to the rumors Perugia was not the simple Italian patriot he pretended to be but the dupe of a gang who sold forgeries of Old Masters to avid South American collectors.

In 1948 the tale was elaborated and authenticated, so it was said, by the deathbed confession of a French marquis, a *marchand amateur,* who claimed to be the brain behind the "gang." One of his clients, a Brazilian millionaire, he said, had repeatedly told him that he would pay anything to possess the *Mona Lisa,* and to satisfy him he had conceived the idea of passing off a perfect copy as the original. To execute the copy, he had a clever forger named André Chandron who had already supplied him with many "Murillos," "Raphaels" and other "great masters." Chandron, however, argued that he could not make a good enough copy without having the original in front of him, and, since the Louvre did not permit copyists, the two conspirators conceived the audacious idea of "borrowing" the masterpiece. Such an action would not only serve the forger's purpose but would lend a very convincing air of verisimilitude to the story they would tell the Brazilian.

According to the marquis, Perugia was hired by him to do the "borrowing" and it was with that sole object that the Italian took his job as a Louvre cleaner. He studied the setup for two months before carrying out the crime and the picture. He hid the picture in his lodgings, where, incredibly, it remained undiscovered while police questioned him there; then it was smuggled to Italy, where during the next two years Chandron produced not one but six copies, all of which were passed off as the original by the marquis to collectors in six different countries.

True or untrue, this extraordinary story has been revived every few years since the marquis's death, usually by someone who claims to have the original *Mona Lisa* for sale. But when I revived it in 1961 it was not, unfortunately, because I had the *Mona Lisa,* or even a "perfect" copy of it, it was simply to anticipate the golden jubilee of the theft. So far as I am aware the *Evening News* was the only newspaper in Great Britain to publish anything to mark the event, but later it appeared that someone else (perhaps an *Evening News* reader?) had decided to mark it in a much more original way. On August 21, the exact anniversary, this someone carried out what several of the following day's newspapers described as "a carbon copy" of the *Mona Lisa* affair, the rape of what became known as "The Goya" from the National Gallery in London. But subsequent events, including the return of the picture in May 1965 and the trial, in November of the same year, in which Kempton Bunton, a sixty-one-year-old unemployed truck driver, was found guilty of stealing the picture's frame (he pleaded successfully that he had only *borrowed* the picture itself), debunked the carbon-copy theory and showed that the culprit's inspiration, although French in origin, was of much more recent date.

At the time when the Goya (a £140,000 portrait of the Duke of Wellington) was stolen an epidemic of major art robberies in France had reached its climax. Early in April 1961 the Colombe d'Or restaurant at St.-Paul-de-Vence, on the Côte d'Azur, famous not only for its doves but also for the remarkable collection of modern paintings that hang in its public rooms, had been relieved of twenty of its most important pictures, among them works by Picasso, Braque, Léger and Chagall. A fortnight later, again at St.-Paul-de-Vence, thieves made another haul, this time of twenty-four modern paintings, valued at £200,000, from the villa of wealthy art dealer Aimé Maeght. But there were bigger things to come.

During the night of July 16 an audacious gang of thieves drove a truck up to the doors of the municipal museum beside the port at St.-Tropez, broke in, loaded almost the entire contents of the former chapel—fifty-seven Impressionist and modern pictures worth half a million pounds—into the truck and drove away without being seen by anyone in the holiday-packed resort. And on the night of August 12–13 (one week before the Goya theft) another gang (or was it the same one?) brought off the most daring art robbery of all when they succeeded in getting away with three quarters of a million pounds' worth of paintings from an exhibition at Aix-en-Provence. The exhibition, of works by Cézanne, who was born and lived at Aix, was in the Pavillon de Vendôme, a beautiful seventeenth-century villa turned museum, where a special guard of two armed policemen had been put on duty for the duration of the show.

Now, in every one of these cases the stolen pictures were subsequently recovered. Those stolen from M. Maeght were found, together with the gang who stole them, within two hours of the robbery. The Colombe d'Or collection was discovered a few weeks later, after the police had been tipped off by a telephone call from a cleric, in the left-luggage office of the Gare St.-Charles in Marseilles. The Cézannes, including the famous *Card Players* from the Louvre and a still life lent by the National Museum of Wales, Cardiff, were missing for eight months before they too were found in Marseilles, abandoned in a stolen car. Again the police had been tipped off by a telephone call. St.-Tropez had to wait twice as long. At the time of the robbery the famous artist Dunoyer de Segonzac, curator of the little *musée,* revealed that the pictures were uninsured. However, he took an opportunist-philosophical view. "Everything will be fine," he said, "and our museum will be famous." But even he had become worried before the police, acting upon information given this time in an anonymous letter, found all but one of the pictures hidden in a barn near a village outside Paris. The single exception was a water color by Dunoyer de Segonzac himself, which had been torn up and returned to him by the thieves. Enraged, no doubt, by the frustration of their plan to demand a ransom from insurers, they intended this act of vandalism as a threat of what would happen to the remainder of the collection if the ransom was not forthcoming from other sources. But although no money was paid and an impudent attempt to sell the pictures to the Ministry of Fine Arts failed, the threat was not carried out. The deterrent, it has been suggested, was the French law which punishes that sort of thing with life imprisonment.

In the press these and the many less spectacular robberies of the same kind that took place not only in Europe but in America as well during 1961 inspired a rash of wild theories propounded in fanciful articles (I wrote some of them myself). Favorite theory, no doubt inspired by the *Mona Lisa* story, was that the robberies were organized by or on behalf of a millionaire maniac collector. One magazine produced a double-page photomontage in color showing this gentleman sitting in a cellar admiring all his recent acquisitions, including the National Gallery's Goya. The *Daily Express,* invoking the spirits of Maigret and Lord Peter Wimsey, went to town. After covering in a few words the theories that ransom money or insurance rewards might be the thieves' motives, a team of "*Express* investigators" reported:

According to an Interpol man in Paris, somewhere in Europe is a Mr. Gloat, whose wealth now lies in art treasures.

Mr. Gloat, it is believed, briefs the thieves, marks down the pictures to be stolen, and then locks them away in his cellar so that he may gloat over them secretly at night. . . .

If the treasures are destined for Mr. Gloat they are already on their way along the old wartime undercover routes that still exist in Europe.

M. Nepote's [Jean Nepote, deputy chief of Interpol] men will be

searching along those routes. They will be watching the Riviera coast
at places like Sète, where wartime agents used to slip in and out.

If those old routes lead to Mr. Gloat, what a perfect finale it would
make for an Inspector Maigret.

An old cobwebby cellar, flickering tallow candles spluttering their
grease on the suit of a man with a magnifying glass and greed on his
face as he looks at the dusty frames.

"Bon soir, mon cher connoisseur," says Maigret, pausing in the en-
trance to fill his pipe. . . .

Good stuff (although I am still wondering why he was looking
at the *frames* with a magnifying glass), but unfortunately the "Mr.
Gloat" theory has little or no basis in fact. Even before the *Daily
Express* article appeared it was well known that in France insurers
had paid ransom money to thieves for the return of stolen paintings, but newspapers were chary of publishing the fact. On August 20, 1961 (the eve of the Goya theft), however, the *Sunday
Telegraph* published a report, datelined Aix-en-Provence, that began: "Insurers have paid ransom secretly to Riviera thieves who
have ransacked art galleries and stolen paintings worth more than
£2 million in the last 20 months. . . ."

By that time the French police were convinced that the big
robberies, at least, were the work of Corsican gangs. In the winter
of 1961 three members of one of the gangs were arrested after
their leader, nicknamed Jean Gros-tête, had been found with four
bullets in his body. The three men were charged with the robbery
at the Colombe d'Or, and three days before Christmas of the
same year each was sentenced to three years' imprisonment; since
then there has been no other major art robbery in the South of
France.

But in the following July London was shocked when a clean-
sweep burglary was made at the O'Hana Gallery. Impressionist
and modern paintings valued at £300,000 or more were taken by

a gang using a van, St.-Tropez style. Immediately a £20,000 reward was offered for information leading to the recovery of the pictures, and two weeks later police "acting on information received" raided an East End warehouse and found them all hidden under a divan. Two men were arrested. When Mr. Jacques O'Hana, the owner of the gallery, heard the news he said, "This is wonderful. The police must be fantastic." But when the two men were brought to trial at the Old Bailey the following January a strange thing happened. The prosecution offered no evidence, the jury were directed to return a verdict of not guilty and the accused were awarded costs and released. And there the matter still rests. No further arrests have been made.

I understand that a reward was paid by the insurers for the information that led the police to the O'Hana pictures. But suggestions in the press that ransom money might be paid in such a case were quickly denied by the British Insurance Association, who stated categorically that no insurance company in Britain would make a private arrangement with a thief for the return of property on payment of a reward. Said the Association:

Insurers make a clear distinction between informers, who run personal risks in passing on information, and thieves and receivers of stolen property who have broken the law. In any case, the rewards are normally offered for information which leads to the recovery of the stolen property *and* the arrest and conviction of the thief or thieves. Moreover, it is usual in this country for rewards to be handed over to informers in the presence of the police.

This high moral attitude of insurance companies springs not only from a desire to discourage the crime of "artnapping" but also from the necessity of keeping within the law. To pay up might lead them to be charged with the crime of misprision of felony. But if this is true how much less likely it is that the

British Government would pay, or agree to the payment of, ransom money. Yet that, apparently, was what Kempton Bunton, the man who took the Goya, had hoped for. He had taken the picture, he said, with the object of helping his campaign for a lower television tax for old-age pensioners.

Evidently, then, we were very fortunate in our artnapper, for it is possible that, just as a kidnapper has been known to kill a child, an artnapper might be driven by fear of arrest to destroy a painting that is too hot to hold. This is what is believed to have happened in 1934 when a panel of the famous polyptych by the van Eyck "brothers" was stolen from the Cathedral of St. Bavon in Ghent and the Belgian Government was held to ransom. The thief, finding that the only response to his first demand was an increase of police activity, sent a second note describing where a part of the panel would be found and threatening destruction of the remainder unless he was paid. According to one report a fragment of the panel was found but when steps were taken to recover the rest, by coming to terms with the thief, nothing more was heard from him and he was later assumed to have died. But in his book *The Pseudo-Arnolfini Portrait* (which, incidentally, attributes the polyptych entirely to Jan van Eyck and convincingly claims that "brother" Hubert is a myth) art historian Maurice Brockwell says that the thief was "the sacristan of an adjoining church turned gambler" and that he collapsed and died when about to confess the details of the theft. Brockwell draws the conclusion that "he had probably long before chopped the panel into small pieces and destroyed the pieces in the fire." However that may be, visitors to the Cathedral of St. Bavon today see a modern copy of the panel, which showed the Just Judges in the procession of the faithful, incorporated in the magnificent fifteenth-century altarpiece.

Artnapping is not, then, a new crime, as was so often said during the epidemic of the early 1960s. In 1876 a portrait, alleged to be of the Duchess of Devonshire and attributed to Gainsborough, was stolen from Agnew's, who had bought it at Christie's a few weeks earlier for the fantastic price of 10,100 guineas (£10,605). Put on show in the firm's new Bond Street gallery, it was the talk of the snob town and thousands went to see it. Then overnight it disappeared. According to one account it was stolen by a notorious American gangster, Adam Worth, who ransomed it for enough money "to end his days in comfort" and was guaranteed immunity from prosecution. But this account is a slur on the British police force, who even then were as rigidly upright in these matters as they are today. A second and more authoritative account is given by A. C. R. Carter,* who relates that the picture was missing for twenty-five years. No money was paid to Worth and no immunity was promised him, so he smuggled it to the United States, where it lay hidden in a Chicago warehouse until he and his accomplices were all dead. In 1901 it was restored to Agnew's, who promptly sold it to Pierpont Morgan for something in the region of £30,000.

The Goya and O'Hana affairs seem now to have had the salutary effect of putting a stop to artnapping, at least in Britain. But if artnapping has stopped, art thefts have not. Thefts from commercial art galleries and sale rooms are almost daily occurrences. Few dealers can have failed to suffer at some time from the pilferers who slip small bronzes, drawings or paintings worth a few hundred pounds into a pocket or a bag as easily as common shoplifters might a packet of tea or a pair of socks. It is all much too easy.

Any regular visitor to the galleries in London's West End frequently finds that he can walk in, spend many minutes looking at an exhibition, and then leave without having seen anyone. Precautions in many galleries are nonexistent. At the height of the

---

* In his book *Let Me Tell You.*

art-crime scare one dealer was displaying a small early Picasso in a glass case, which could easily have been opened with a pen-knife, outside his gallery. Asked if he took the picture in at night he said, "Oh, no, it's insured. The insurance companies make the jewelers round here empty their windows at night, but not us." In fact, insurers in Britain were not greatly perturbed by the epidemic. Jewelry was, and still is, a far worse risk for them than works of art. Yet in the South of France Mr. Somerset Maugham had decided to sell his collection because the burden of complying with insurance regulations outweighed the pleasure he took in it.

Today in London the small-time thieves are a more serious problem than the big men. Many of them are victims of the contagious disease of art collecting—incipient kleptomaniacs crazed with envy by the daily reports of fantastic prices paid for "priceless" works of art. (A classic example of this type was the young Yugoslav house painter whose home, an attic room in Paris, was found in 1963 to be stacked with nearly half a million pounds' worth of paintings, drawings and antiques.) A second category are common criminals of the type who would steal jam jars if the price of jam jars suddenly boomed. They have no special knowledge of art or how to dispose of their loot and usually make the mistake of asking far too little when they try to sell. A third and much more dangerous group are those with some considerable knowledge of art and of the art market, the sort of small fry and hangers-on who insinuate themselves into the auction rings, and the knockers and con men who operate on the fringe of the art game.

Even now, when it is well known that men who steal masterpieces almost invariably have ransom in mind, newspapers seldom fail to follow up the big art-robbery story with warnings to the thieves that they will never be able to sell the pictures. But although the major works of major artists are too well documented for a thief's safety, he can, like the forger of today, do very well out of very minor things. At the lower levels of the great hierarchy of collectors are thousands of people who will pay one or two hundred pounds for almost anything with a good name attached to it. Every day dealers and auctioneers are being offered minor works that are not recorded anywhere, and unless their suspicions are aroused by the seller's behavior there is no reason why they should not accept them. Sometimes a dealer or auctioneer who has been robbed will circularize the trade with details of missing items, probably to comply with insurance requirements, but little is done to *prevent* thefts. And indeed, short of taking the elaborate, expensive and electronic closing-the-stable-door-after-the-horse-has-gone sort of precautions that were taken at the National Gallery, there is not much that can be done to stop the professional thief. But at the moment security in most museums and dealers' galleries is so poor that the temptation to the amateur thief and the kleptomaniac is irresistible.

13

Instant
Artists

*Art's "three thousand odd rules" can-
not be learned by the "ten thousand
creatures." Anybody cannot be an
artist.*
—Ad Reinhardt,
"The Next Revolution in Art"

*Let everyone make himself an ama-
teur.*
—Clive Bell,
Art

You may wonder why, in this book, I have left the artist until last.
The reason is simple. In the art game he is the least important
player. I am speaking, of course, of the living artist, who, as we
have already seen, is considered by most dealers to be a risky investment who has to be subsidized by the profits made out of
dead artists. No major London gallery (with the possible exception of Marlborough Fine Art, which has such best sellers as
Henry Moore, Ben Nicholson, Graham Sutherland, Francis Bacon,
Barbara Hepworth and Oskar Kokoschka in its "stable") could
survive on the proceeds of exhibitions by living British artists

alone. The cost of operating in the West End of London is so high that the proprietor of a modest-sized gallery off Bond Street told me that he would have to sell an average of at least £2,000 a week (at 33⅓ per cent commission) if he was to devote himself entirely to living British artists. To do that he would have to have good selling exhibitions running throughout the year, and this is almost impossible. In any case it would be very hard work. Much easier to sell a minor picture by a well-known dead artist, an Impressionist or Post-Impressionist maybe, and make a thousand or two that way.

No need, then, to waste sympathy on the gallery proprietor who has a flop exhibition on his hands; if he is any sort of dealer at all he has probably just unloaded, in the back room, some dead man's picture at a nice, big, fat profit. But what of the artist, the living artist? Not a Sutherland or a Nicholson, nor even a David Hockney or a Bridget Riley, but a Bill Brown who is a very good painter, is around thirty and has never had a one-man show before. He left the Royal College of Art six years ago after having studied there and at an ordinary art school for a total of eight years. Since then he has struggled along, refusing to become a commercial artist but doing one day's teaching a week at an art school for, say, £12 a day.

His show is a success. Not a sensational success, but a prestige success. They do not talk about him on the BBC's *Critics* program or write about him in the gossip columns of the popular newspapers, but the genuine critics praise his work. He sells eighteen pictures, just over half the total. Unfortunately they are mostly the small pictures, and the average price works out at £60. After the gallery has taken its commission there is £720 due to the artist. Then the proprietor of the gallery agrees to keep four of the unsold pictures for stock and very generously pays half price for them in cash. This gives Brown a total of £900. Suddenly he feels rich. Of course, he does not get all the money at once—some customers take a long time to pay—but he will probably get it all within six months. In the meantime he could pay the framing bill for the exhibition, £170 (it is important to have good frames, the dealer had told him). And he could pay his outstanding bill for materials, £35 (about a quarter of what he has spent preparing for the exhibition). There is, he remembers, a year's rent for his studio to take into account and there will be income tax to pay later. Suddenly he does not feel rich any more. He will, he reckons, have made rather less than £200 net for rather more than a year's work. Even so he is lucky. At another gallery he might have had to pay part of the costs of the catalogue and of the private-view party. What is more, he has been promised another exhibition in two years' time. By then, he hopes, his pictures will have gone up a little in price and he will probably (but equally probably he will not) sell more. He might even make £500! There is another possibility, too, that he dreams of. He may be talent-spotted by Marlborough Fine Art, who will take him into their stable, double his prices, treble his sales, take fifty per cent commission and make him a rich man. But at that same moment 9,999 other good artists are having exactly the same dream.

There are far more galleries in London now than there were before the war at which a young artist might hope to get a one-man show; but the competition is also much greater, and, although no artist need starve now (unless the idiot insists on being a "pure" artist), it is a mistake to think that because art is booming all artists are doing very nicely, thank you. It is a rat race like any other business today, and luck and influence and publicity (especially publicity) rather than talent can often be the tickets to financial success. In the past decade we have witnessed not only the tremendous influence of the *painting* of the New York school but also the tremendous influence of the self-advertising, self-promoting, self-sensationalizing methods of the artists of the New York school. Most of the Browns of British art, dedicated, serious, trained professional artists, have seen those galleries that they aspired to being repeatedly filled with the work of inferior professional artists, with superior selling techniques, who have sold themselves on the strength of some secondhand, imported gimmick. There is, however, another type of gallery-space consumer whom the Browns find even harder to stomach: the instant artist.

For centuries there was only one way to become an artist—the hard way. To anyone who is seriously contemplating becoming a serious artist it may be of interest here to quote a brief summary of what "the hard way" means which was given to Harvard students by the American artist Ben Shahn:

Attend a university if you possibly can. There is no content of knowledge that is not pertinent to the work you will want to do. But before you attend a university work at something for a while. Do anything. Get a job in a potato field; or work as a grease-monkey in an auto repair shop. But if you do work in a field do not fail to observe the look and the feel of earth and of all things that you handle—yes, even potatoes! Or, in the auto shop, the smell of oil and grease and burning rubber. Paint, of course, but if you have to lay aside painting for a time, continue to draw. Listen well to all conversations and be instructed by them and take all seriousness seriously. Never look down upon anything or anyone as not worthy of notice. In college or out of college, read. And form opinions! Read Sophocles and Euripides and Dante and Proust. Read everything that you can find about art except the reviews. Read the Bible; read Hume; read *Pogo*. Read all kinds of poetry and know many poets and many artists. Go to an art school, or two, or three, or take art courses at night if necessary. And paint and paint and draw and draw. Know all that you can, both curricular and noncurricular—mathematics and physics and economics, logic, and particularly history. Know at least two languages besides your own, but anyway, know French. Look at pictures and more pictures. Look at every kind of visual symbol, every kind of emblem; do not spurn signboards or furniture drawings or this style of art or that style of art.

Do not be afraid to like paintings honestly or to dislike them honestly, but if you do dislike them retain an open mind. Do not dismiss any school of art, not the Pre-Raphaelites nor the Hudson River School nor the German Genre painters. Talk and talk and sit at cafés, and listen to everything, to Brahms, to Brubeck, to the Italian hour on the radio. Listen to preachers in small town churches and in big city churches. Listen to politicians in New England town meetings and to rabble-rousers in Alabama. Even draw them. And remember that you are trying to learn to think what you want to think, that you are trying to co-ordinate mind and hand and eye. Go to all sorts of museums and galleries and to the studios of artists. Go to Paris and Madrid and Rome and Ravenna and Padua. Stand alone in Sainte Chapelle, in the Sistine Chapel, in the Church of the Carmine in Florence. Draw and paint and learn to work in many media; try lithography and aquatint and silk-screen. Know all that you can about art, and by all means have opinions. Never be afraid to become embroiled in art or life or politics; never be afraid to learn to draw or paint better than you already do; and never be afraid to undertake any kind of art at all, however exalted or however common, but do it with distinction.*

But in the age of the ready-mix and the prefab a new phenomenon appeared—the instant artist. In a world in which there were already far too many artists, even good ones, the idea grew up that anyone can be an artist. When Clive Bell wrote, before the First World War: "Art must become less exclusively professional. That will not be achieved by bribing the best artists to debase themselves, but by enabling everyone to create such art as he can"† no one, mercifully, took much notice of him. But in more recent years the idea was reiterated so often by otherwise responsible and intelligent people (including Sir Winston Churchill, who, by his example and with his delightful book *Painting as a*

---

* Ben Shahn, "The Education of an Artist," in *The Shape of Content.*
† Clive Bell, *Art.*

Pastime, did more than any other individual to spread the paint-ing bug) that it caught on and spread like a plague. Suddenly everyone seemed to be painting—Cabinet ministers, field mar-shals, royal dukes, duchesses, debutantes and dustmen, Mrs. Mopps, bank clerks, fish porters, housewives and chimpanzees.

Inevitably this was hailed by art educationists and others who ought to have known better as proof of a tremendous upsurge of interest in art. It was nothing of the sort. On the contrary, in ninety-nine cases out of a hundred the amateur dauber becomes so enamored of his own pettifogging efforts that he is completely blind to art. The only gainers from his activities (unless we regard his self-satisfaction as a gain) are the manufacturers of artists' ma-terials and the army of self-appointed art teachers who suddenly appeared to meet the demand for quick ways to become an artist.

The advertisements of some of these teachers reveal the fatuous nature of this "great upsurge of interest in art." Here, for instance, is a passage from an advertisement for a learn-to-paint-by-post course:

What does he teach? V—— is an Impressionist: his teaching also is based on Impressionism. He throws perpective, anatomy, composition, out of his studio window. "I am concerned," he says, "only with mak-ing this blank canvas look like my subject." Accordingly his exercises teach observation and analysis of tone and colour. His students learn to accept objects as pure optical sensations to be transmitted to canvas with growing accuracy as the course progresses.

And here is the advertisement of a "teacher" offering practical lessons:

You want to be an artist? Write to James W——. Within a week you can be taking lessons in oil painting, learning Impressionism and producing a good picture.

It is curious how many of such teachers refer to themselves as Impressionists (with a capital *I*) and talk of Impressionism as though it were the apogee of painting. For them the history of art, having reached its highest manifestation about 1880, has stood still ever since. It is the most widely held idea about art of all, but it will not last much longer, not simply because it is not true but because the diminishing supply of genuine Impressionist paintings will make it unnecessary and undesirable. With all the worthwhile Impressionist pictures locked up inside museums, the art market will be obliged to select a new apogee the manifestations of which are still in fairly plentiful supply.

Mr. John Wynne-Morgan, probably the most successful businessman among these self-appointed "Impressionist" teachers, once told me, "I loathe abstract painting and I loathe action painting." And in one of his books, *Oil Painting as a Pastime*, he says of the first, "I frankly just don't understand it," and of the second, "To my mind it is beneath contempt and unworthy of comment." Fair enough. He is not alone in those sentiments. But when he writes a few pages later that drawing "is a bogey from the past" and that lack of knowledge of draftsmanship could, in some cases, be an advantage, he is talking very like an action painter himself. Mr. Wynne-Morgan conducts his painting lessons both by correspondence and in his studio. In a brochure advertising the former it is claimed: "If you follow his teaching conscientiously, he guarantees to make you an artist." That is going too far. To have legions of amateur daubers going around calling themselves artists is preposterous. Yet that is what is happening. They are the instant artists.

In fact I do not object to amateur artists (I agree rather with Degas that there are no amateur artists, only good and bad ones), but I find that exhibitions of the work of "hobby artists" and "pastime artists" hold no more interest for me than exhibitions of fretwork. Unfortunately we are still a long way from Clive

Bell's dream. "Once it is understood," he said, "that art which is unfit for public exhibition may yet be created for private pleasure, no one will feel shame at being called an amateur." The trouble today is that an enormous proportion of the hundreds of thousands of amateurs (500,000 in Britain, according to recent estimates) are not content with what Sir Winston Churchill called "a joy ride in a paintbox." Most of them do not consider their efforts unfit for public exhibition but insist upon parading them before us in crass, jumbo-size "art" shows that come round with remorseless regularity year after year. Even worse, more and more of them are dropping their amateur status and muscling in on the art game. (This could be your way in, but it depends on who you are.)

In recent years we have seen in London galleries a succession of one-man shows by actors and actresses, Cabinet ministers, comedians and countesses, debutantes, duchesses and doctors, nearly all of which were sellouts. On rare occasions a dustman or a fish porter or a chimpanzee was given a show, but it was usually found that they did not have the sort of friends who would come along and buy their pictures. The most popular type of instant artist was (a) female, (b) young, (c) pretty, (d) the daughter of a peer or a millionaire or both, (e) bored with debutante balls, boys, being a model or writing novels. She was a gift to the gossip columnists, who printed big pictures of her with captions that went something like this:

Artist Lavinia

Former model the Hon. Lavinia Pinxit-Hyphen-Plumket, Lord Plonk's daughter, who has been in Spain writing a novel, has returned to London to become an artist.

"While on the beach at Torremolinos," she said at her parents' Mayfair home, "the famous Spanish artist Pedro Amorino saw me drawing in the sand with my toes and told me I have a natural talent. He has offered me free tuition. It's all frightfully exciting."

Already she is planning her first exhibition—in the autumn at the Upper Upper Gallery.

"I think," said Lavinia, "that I will be an abstract artist like Amorino. He's the most marvellous man."

Lavinia had her exhibition. Daddy (who probably paid for the hire of the gallery) and Mummy and their friends went along and bought up all her "abstractions," and thereafter the gossip columns of the daily papers referred to her as "artist Lavinia Pinxit-Hyphen-Plumket."

The determined and well-heeled go-getter (who is seldom a good artist) can always get himself or herself an exhibition somewhere in London, for apart from a few galleries at which rooms can be hired there are scores of clubs, restaurants and hotels that will provide hanging space. Not long ago I was conned into visiting an exhibition of a collection of execrable paintings by a wealthy young amateur artist who told me that he was planning to give up a promising career in his father's business and devote himself entirely to painting. I asked him if he would be going to art school. "Oh no," he said. "I have been advised by Sir Herbert Read not to because it would destroy my natural talent for expressing myself spontaneously." I find it very hard to believe that Sir Herbert Read said anything of the sort, but I quote the incident here because it illustrates a widely held illusion that, *pace* Clive Bell, I believe to be nonsense.

The idea that art is "expressing oneself spontaneously" is a heresy that has given rise only to a vast flood of rubbish, a flood even greater than that provoked by the Victorian heresy that art was "copying nature" and the Impressionist heresy that it was "recording the image received by the retina." All three *can* be art, but only when a true artist does them, and then only because an artist is incapable of spontaneous expression, copying or recording in the sense understood, or rather misunderstood, by the instant artist. For, as Ernst Fischer has put it:

> In order to be an artist it is necessary to seize, hold, and transform experience into memory, memory into expression, material into form. Emotion for an artist is not everything . . . the passion that consumes the dilettante serves the true artist. . . . The free play of art is the result of mastery.*

"True artist," "mastery"—such terms have a curiously old-fashioned ring about them. Today art is like an all-in wrestling match in which the winner is often the one who puts on the most bizarre show. The mentality of the instant artist is not confined to amateurs. The art student straight from school is encouraged by the commercial setup to regard himself as a finished artist, to splurge his immature libido across a series of outsize canvases in the hope that they will attract attention to him. In his Harvard lecture Shahn said that for a serious artist recognition is only the wine of his repast, its substance is the accomplishment of the work itself. But today most student painters on leaving our art colleges go straight for the wine and to hell with the substance. In a world in which recognition can be won without accomplishment why should they bother about accomplishment?

What is accomplishment, anyway? Art is anything that an artist produces. The student has this not only on the authority of established artists (e.g. Robert Rauschenberg's "It is art because I say it is" and F. N. Souza's "Art is what I do") but on the authority of the art market in which two bus tickets stuck together by Kurt Schwitters or a straight line signed "Picasso" are each worth enough to keep an Indian family from starvation for ten years. No wonder the idea of being able to call himself an artist appeals to the student (and to the amateur) so much. It is a pass-

---

* Ernst Fischer, *The Necessity of Art*.

port to do any crazy thing he likes and expect to be paid, or at any rate admired, for doing it.

There may be no short cuts to becoming an artist, but today there are plenty of short cuts to becoming known as an artist, which, generally, is a far more lucrative achievement. Never before has the climate of art been more conducive to charlatanism. For every genuine artist who succeeds in getting a one-man show in London there are half a dozen phonies, not only idiot-amateurs and dilettanti but also those art-college-trained slickers whose principal talent is for recognizing a bandwagon as soon as it appears and climbing on it smartly, the sort of artistic wideboy whose work Joyce Cary must have had in mind when he put into the mouth of Gulley Jimson those immortal words of criticism, "It's like farting 'Annie Laurie' through a keyhole; very clever, but not art." In New York and Paris the ratio of the phony to the sincere is even greater, much greater, and the general impression given to the poor layman is that the whole of contemporary art is a vast sham.

14

The
Next
Revolution

*As people with ambition and
ability, we do not want to furnish
some museum, however successful
we may be. That is why we have
entered the field of public art.*
—JOHN BOWSTEAD,
BERNARD JENNINGS,
ROGER JEFFS, TERRY ATKINSON,
Fine Artz Associates,
manifesto in *Ark.*

*What immense innovations are
being wrought all around us now
. . . how can artists portray it all
with the old means of art?*
—BERTOLT BRECHT,
"Formalism"

*The art to come will be the con-
cretion in form of a scientific
conviction.*
—FRANZ MARC,
Aphorism 35

One day in 1962 I was looking through the *Daily Telegraph,* to
find what its critic had to say about an exhibition I had seen him
at the day before, when the headline "Pop Art" caught my eye and
I began to read what appeared to be a review of the work of an
artist, John Gasby, of whom I had never heard. Although it was
not what I was looking for, I was compelled, after the first few
lines, to read on:

Gasby's latest works, making use of a metaphysical pullulation of
disparate forms, painted surfaces, false beards, oscillographs, chewed-

up telephones, Victorian daguerrotypes smeared with treacle and disinfectant, collapsed bedsteads and mummified rats, not only express
the existential violence of the urban junkscape. They actually *are* vio-
lent in themselves.

Parts of his enormous compositions are cunningly sown with land-
mines or booby-trapped in such a way that the unwary art-lover may
be dropped 30 feet into a pit of quicklime. In other parts fierce
Tibetan mastiffs are chained up or there are wardrobes full of lead
poised to fall at a touch.

The fear of sudden death or serious injury, and indeed the actual
experience of these things, Gasby believes, is today an essential part
of the aesthetic experience, impacting a tonal sporadicism, a uni-
versalized fragmentalism which has revolutionized our fundamental
concepts of meaning, function and image.

Gasby has all the artist's perpetual impulse to move on to new forms,
new experiments. After completing a new work, he tells me, he always
keeps well away from it himself.

How much of that, I wonder, did you have to read before you
realized that it was a "cod" review? Probably very little. Yet I,
who had the advantage of knowing that it was part of the satirical
"Way of the World" column by "Peter Simple," have to admit that
it was not until I reached the bit about land mines that I was sure
it was meant to be funny. This is no reflection upon my sense of
humor, nor, indeed, upon Peter Simple's. The fact is that that first
paragraph reads very much like hundreds of "serious" reviews
that have appeared in recent years. Such phrases as "pullulation of
disparate forms" and "violence of the urban junkscape" are virtually standard critical language, as we have seen in Chapter
Eleven. But that is not all. Anyone who has followed the three-
ring circus that is avant-garde art today will know that artists do
make use of false beards, oscillographs, chewed-up telephones,
Victorian daguerrotypes, collapsed (and uncollapsed) bedsteads,
and mummified rats. And if they thought the publicity would help

they would not hesitate to cover the whole lot with treacle and disinfectant.

The truth is that there is hardly any object that a professional humorist like Peter Simple, or anyone else for that matter, can think of that has not already been used by the so-called New Realists or Neo-Dadaists. Glancing through a single back number of *Art International,* picked at random, I find illustrations of paintings, collages, constructions and sculptures incorporating the following things: a tree, a double divan, an electric toaster, a commode, a bath, a lawn mower, a stag's head, a stuffed hawk and a handsaw (just to show the artist knows the difference?), paper flowers, a doll, a gas mask, glass eyes, pills, birds' eggs, apples, ampoules, pins, ping-pong balls, a wineglass, soap, a comb, wire netting, string, chair legs, door handles, a window, a sugar bowl, tables and chairs, a complete bathroom (with towels, laundry basket, bathmat, electric-light switch and cut-out nude), false teeth, a gas stove, etc., etc., etc.

And still that is not all. Reading about Gasby's belief that the actual experience of sudden death or serious injury is today "an essential part of the aesthetic experience" recalled for me a meeting I had with a member of the Parisian "Happenings Movement," Ben Vauthier. At that time Mr. Vauthier and his wife were living in the window of London's Gallery One in full view of passers-by. They were one of the exhibits in an exhibition called "The Misfits," which included, among other things, a reproduction of the *Mona Lisa,* with large nails sticking out of it; below it was a vegetable rack complete with an assortment of vegetables and a notice inviting visitors to take a carrot, a beetroot, a cabbage or a potato and slam it onto the *Mona Lisa.* Another exhibit was a "magic box" which Mr. Vauthier tried to sell me at what he called the bargain price of twenty pounds. It was a small, roughly made wooden box painted black and containing some object or objects that rattled when it was shaken. The "magic" lay in the fact that as long as the box remained unopened its contents would remain a mystery compelling curiosity!

Mr. Vauthier explained that the exhibition was rather small beer compared with some of the things he and his friends had "made happen" in Paris. There was, for example, the time they filled an art gallery from floor to ceiling with refuse from the city's dust carts. But what intrigued me most were his stories of Yves Klein, the archpriest of happenings, who, he said, was then missing, believed dead. For a long time Mr. Klein had planned a supreme happening in which he was to be run over by a steamroller, but when he tried to make it happen in a Paris street the police intervened. He was, they said, causing a traffic jam. In fact Yves Klein is now dead. He died not dramatically under a steamroller but of conventional "natural causes."

In America too "death and serious injury" have occupied the minds of a section of the avant-garde during the past few years. The Gertrude Stein Gallery in New York held an exhibition called "American Death Show" and another called the "No-Show." A brochure issued in connection with the latter called for "art that screams, roars, vomits, rages, goes mad, murders, rapes, commits every bloody and obscene act it can to express only a shred of the human emotions that lie prisoner beneath the sanitary tiles here in adman's utopia." New York also had its own share of happenings, one of which was called (but only after it had happened, because happenings don't have titles) A Service for the Dead and was created in the boiler room of the Maidman Playhouse. The place, a huge, cavernous pit, reeked of oil fumes and the smell of rot. Water gurgled across the floor, and from the ceiling hung clusters of garbage cans, buckets and other junk, which were clanked together at intervals to augment a dirge played by a group of "bum"-musicians. Below the garbage cans a ladder was suspended horizontally by four ropes. On it a nude girl lay motionless, her hands across her breasts as if in death. Lights flashed on and off, sirens shrieked and wailed, a woman giggled hysterically. Suddenly out of darkness flashlights picked out the "dead" girl on the ladder, which was swaying over the heads of the on-lookers. Then suddenly the "corpse" flung out her arms and scattered handfuls of torn papers over the people below.

This sort of thing belongs properly to the theater, of course, but the man who devised it, Allan Kaprow, had been a painter, and he has explained how it developed from collages and assemblages he had made "using painted paper, cloth and photos, as well as mirrors, electric lights, plastic film, aluminum foil, ropes, straw; objects that could be attached to, or hung in front of, the canvas along with various sounds and odors."

Kaprow is only one of hundreds of serious artists who, in the twenty years since the end of World War II, have abandoned paints and brushes as a means of expression, who believe that the art of the "easel-weasel" is played out, finished. There is nothing new in this. The Dadaists said the same thing nearly fifty years ago and the Neo-Dadaists, the New Realists, the Pop artists, etc., in spite of their protests to the contrary, have in effect simply carried on where the old brigade left off. In the same way, the happenings-makers have merely carried to their illogical conclusions ideas which the Surrealists were experimenting with forty years ago. Both groups are, in fact, neoromantics whose days are already numbered. Nevertheless, like action painting and the craze for the jumbo-size canvas that it initiated, they provided a few more nails for the coffin of the reactionary cult-of-the-precious-object-in-the-gilt-frame which is the principal foundation of the art game. They are symptoms of a revolution that must ultimately succeed in spite of all the counterrevolutionary rear-guard actions we, the art-gamesmen, may fight.

That there are probably more easel pictures being painted today than ever before does not alter the fact that this form of art has been dying for fifty years. The present vast quantity being vomited forth may even be the final death throe. Ninety-nine-point-nine recurring per cent of them will be absolutely valueless in a hundred years' time. The remainder will probably have found their way into the public art galleries to fill the last gaps in the completed history of easel painting which will have lasted six hundred years. To a not-far-distant-future generation those great art galleries (called "museums" even in Britain by then) will be of no more interest to the general public than the museums of palaeontology or ethnography. The art-gamesman's dream of educating the masses to appreciate the precious-object sort of art will long ago have been abandoned, along with the art galleries, to a handful of square eggheads. The masses will have their own sort of art all around them. What sort of art will it be? It will not be anything like the bulk of what passes for avant-garde art today. Not only will the brush-and-paint tradition have been finally played out; with it into oblivion will have gone the rubbish collages made by the legions of would-be neo-Schwitterses, all the old-iron sculptures of imitation Tinguelys, all the drip paintings of imitation Pollocks, the squashed motorcars of John Chamberlain, the outsize prize-winning doodles of Messrs. Hilton and Mundy, the dust-laden combine paintings of Rauschenberg and company, the giant baked-potato and hamburger jokes of Claes Oldenburg, the latter-day ready-mades of Mr. Jim Dine and his followers, the burned books of Mr. John Latham, the burned canvases of Herr Otto Piene and the slashed and torn ones of Signor Fontana and Señor Millares.

It was all fun, even exciting fun, while it lasted, but it was mostly marking time or, at best, consolidating the discoveries of an earlier generation. It was also a jamboree for pseudo innovators. Peggy Guggenheim (whose collection of "modern art" has been described as second to none in private hands) wrote in 1960, not without some justification, that art had gone to hell—not permanently, of course. "One cannot expect every decade to produce genius," she said. "The twentieth century has already produced enough. A field must lie fallow now and then. Artists try too hard to be original. That is why we have all this painting that isn't painting any more."*

On reflection, what a very curious statement that is for Miss Guggenheim to have made. Evidently the great champion of the avant-garde of the 1940s has become the reactionary of the 1960s, unable to accept that the day will come when painting as we know it will be practiced, if at all, only as a quaint antique revival, in somewhat the same way as morris dancing survives today. Far from being finished or lying fallow, the art of the twentieth century is now working toward a revolution far greater than that with which it began. In the apparent chaos of today's art the germ of the new art is pulsating. In failing to detect it Miss Guggenheim has aligned herself with the layman, who, although he makes no objection to being rushed along by science that he doesn't understand, demands that art should dawdle along with him, explaining itself as it goes. To say that we have "painting that isn't painting any more" because artists are trying too hard to be original is the wrong answer to the wrong question. The only artists who are trying to be original are the spurious artists who are no more a part of the vital body of living art than are those "artists" who, in the second half of the twentieth century, produce "Impressionist" landscapes. The genuine artist does not strive to be original, he is original involuntarily. If he is young his originality may well take a form that people of Miss Guggenheim's generation, or of mine, find difficult to accept. But rather than accuse the artist of insincerity, of "trying too hard," we should acknowledge that if only because of his youth his art is probably nearer in spirit to the art of the future than we are.

Experience ought to have taught us that in the technological age into which we are now being pushed art will be at least as different from the art of Miss Guggenheim's beloved old men— Picasso, Ernst, Miró—as theirs was from that of their grandfathers'

---

* Peggy Guggenheim, *Confessions of an Art Addict.*

day. We are still inclined today to regard the artist's use of uncon-
ventional materials as a gimmick, and so in many cases it undoubtedly is. But there is in this search for new materials a strong
pointer to the fundamental way in which the art of the future will
differ from that of the present. Technology has already made
available to the artist a great variety of new media, and it is in
these and, no doubt, the many more to come that the art of the
technological age will be created. According to the four young
ex-Slade ex-painters who provided the quotation that heads this
chapter:

We've had the push-button revolution and the technological take-
over. We've been presented with conveyor-belt production, cyber-
netics, depth psychology, mass communication, instant-packs, super-
markets, glam admanship, man-made fibres, neon, nylon, perspex,
plastic, expanding economics and dynamic obsolescence. It's all there
—miraculous materials, magical machines, communication techniques
and more leisure. And how can the visual artist serve in this social
clime? He can avail himself of all these fabulous facilities and use
his creative intelligence and imagination to produce inventive and desirable objects, environments and atmospheres. In fact, supply a visual
panorama in this new Golden Age in which culture can fulfil its real
function and enhance and stimulate the non-functional leisure-time of
society.*

Presumably the "inventive and desirable objects" will include
not only the motor scooters and electric guitars of the teenagers
who, the Fine Artz quartet remind us, are the general public of
tomorrow, but also such things as the electrically operated and
uncanny mobile sculptures of the Belgian Pol Bury and the mag-
netically controlled, gravity-defying objects of the Greek sculptor
Takis. The "environments and atmospheres" would include the
luminodynamic constructions of the Hungarian-born French

* *Ark,* No. 35 (1964).

sculptor Nicholas Schöffer, the "luminous pictures" of the English inventor John Healey and the "robot pictures" of P. K. Hoenich. There would be, too, no doubt, examples of the "random art," pioneered by the Italians "Group T" of Milan and "Group N" of Padua, in which iron filings, ping-pong balls, plastic ribbons and other objects are activated electronically.

In all these things, it will be noted, the accent is on movement. Fifty-five years ago the Futurists were attempting to express in paint the sensation of motion, but later artists bypassed this problem and offered the spectator real motion in somewhat the same way as Picasso and Braque, realizing the futility of painting imitation wood and newspapers in their still lifes, stuck pieces of wood-patterned wallpaper and scraps of newspaper onto their canvases and so pioneered what has become the elaborate arts of collage and constructivism. The desire for motion in art goes much deeper than that of a few avant-gardists looking for a new gimmick that brings them publicity. The development of moving sculpture from the first mobiles of Alexander Calder, thirty-five years ago, and the development of light-pictures since the attempts, still earlier in the century, to create "color music" will be regarded by the twenty-first century as the most important contributions made to art in the twentieth, not even excluding Cubism.

What was thought by most of us to be the mumbo-jumbo of a few young exhibitionists when, a few years ago, we first heard talk of environmental art and saw exhibitions, with names like "Situation" and "Place," which enveloped us in a maze of outside canvases will be seen to have been prophetic. But instead of a temporary environment of painted canvases there will be an everyday environment in which there are moving sculptures on every street corner, vast ever-changing color abstractions projected on the sides of great buildings (and on the insides too, as an alternative or accompaniment to stereophonic music while we relax), electronic "perpetual-motion" machines to entertain us at the air-bus stop and at the Channel Tunnel stations, electromagnetic art objects in the hospital waiting rooms (we shall always have *them*) to induce a hypnotic calm in the patient waiting to have a worn-out limb replaced or a new brain grafted. The passion for movement will also spread to architecture. Changeable interiors will have been combined with changeable exteriors. Buildings constructed on the Ferris-wheel principle will ensure that the computer minder in his office or the button presser in the factory will never have the same view out of his window for more than a few consecutive minutes.

If this new world does not appeal to you it is probably because you are too old. But if, as has been said, the clues to tomorrow's culture lie in the cults of today, it will appeal to the next-but-one generation of people your age, the generation that has been brought up from birth on television and atomic energy, space travel and electronics, purple hearts and beat music, to whom silence is leaden and not to move is to be dead. Theirs, the Fine Artz men tell us, will be a "fab, kandy-coloured, leisure-loving, kustom-built-for-comfort, super-styled and slickline, bright new world."

You are glad you will not be here to see it? But this is only the immediate future. Many artists today are looking much further ahead. The sculptor Constant Nieuwenhuys, for example, visualizes a world (see illustration section following page 96) in which,

since all the work will be done by machines, the new man will be free to spend his life, like a nomad, travelling through the ever changing New Babylon and sampling some of the intense and gratifying experiences it will provide. The energies now devoted to work will be spent on the development of man's creative capacities in the world-wide city, which will be a sort of enormous playground. It will consist basically of flexible living sectors with open spaces in between for parks, agricultural lands and gardens, covering the entire surface of the earth. The environment will alter according to the desires and activities of the passing *Homo ludens*. In this flux of change and movement the common creative force will create a collective mood and atmosphere (something like collective poetry), which will be both the aim and the justification of the life of this new nomadic race.*

What will happen to art as we move forward to this New Babylon? Opinions differ. To those who believe that art is a substitute for something lacking in life, a religion, a sublimation of a desire that is not directly satisfied, it seems logical to suppose that in an ideal world art (like the State in Marx's ideal Communism) will wither away. That great pioneer of abstract art Piet Mondrian expressed this when he said, "Art will disappear as life gains more equilibrium." But the idea is challenged, surprisingly enough perhaps, by the Marxist philosopher Ernst Fischer. He rejects the belief that art is only a substitute and encouragingly asserts that "art was not merely necessary in the past but will always remain so." On the other hand, if it is true that, as Fischer puts it, "an artist can only experience something which his time and his social conditions have to offer" and "even the most subjective artist works on behalf of society," it is certain that the art of the New Babylon will be vastly different from anything we know today. The several arts will no longer be separated from each other or from science. Art, with a capital A, will be collectively created for collective delectation.

So much for speculation. Yet one thing we may be sure of—that the art game as we know it, the "personal art-dealing, private art-collecting and individual artist-enterprising of personalistic, privateering art" will disappear as life gains more equilibrium. But keep calm. There is no need yet for alarm, all you actual and would-be collectors, investors, dealers, runners, knockers, auctioneers, experts, critics, art historians, museum wallahs, art-gossipmongers, forgers, fakers, fiddlers, publicists, phony art teachers, culture hawkers and innumerable other art-etceteras. The New

---

* *ICA Bulletin,* No. 140 (October 1964).

Babylon won't be coming for a long, long time. When? Poet
Stanley Brouwn puts it (pessimistically, I think) at

> 4000 A.D.
> When Science and Art are entirely
> Melted together to something new
> When the people will have lost their
> Remembrance and thus will have
> No past, only future.
> When they will have to discover everything
> Every moment again and again
> When they will have lost their need for
> Contact with others . . .
> . . . Then they will live in a world of only
> Colour, Light, Space, Time, Sounds and Movement
> Then colour light space time
> Sounds and movement will be free
> No Music
> No Theatre
> No Art
> No
> There will be SOUND
> > COLOUR
> > LIGHT
> > SPACE
> > TIME
> > MOVEMENT

Constant Nieuwenhuys, however, believes that the nonworking
society will come sooner than most people expect and that it is
sufficiently near for artists and others to be doing something about
it now. The specific task of the creative man of today is "to pre-
pare a new exciting reality based on the actual possibilities of
technical production, instead of depicting and expressing the
unsatisfying and stagnant reality that is about to be liquidated."
Any activity in the field of art that is not already concerned with
this *Homo ludens* can already be called backward.

Epilogue:

Will
the
Boom
Last?

When I wrote in Chapter One that "the knowledge that the present boom cannot last forever will give him [the art-gamesman] a sense of urgency" I had in mind what might be called, more or less literally, the money-for-old-rope aspect of the boom. Shortly before, a friend had been telling me of a conversation he had with a New York dealer who handles the work of several modern American artists but who confessed that he would never buy back anything he had sold. The reason the dealer gave was that the works of these artists would not last, not even in the physical sense. My friend, an artist who uses traditional oil-painting techniques to make pictures "that will last a thousand years," was

shocked. The unkind thought that it might be better for everyone if the greater part of all contemporary art were nondurable
seems not to have occurred to him. Nor does he seem to have
been able to accept the idea of expendable art—i.e., a work of art
created to last only a strictly limited period of time, a moment,
or a month, or more, or less. Yet it is one of the most significant
features of the art boom of the 1960s that there is, especially in
America, a market for expendable art. (In a country where the
economy is based upon expendability of all commodities, why
should art be excepted?)

Whereas in the past the buyer of a painting or sculpture took it
for granted that the work was durable (he was not always right,
but that is by the way), today there are "collectors" who, for reasons ranging from crude publicity-seeking to a genuine (if mis-
guided) belief that they are contributing something to the future
of art, pay large sums for some piece of nonsense that on its brief
journey from the dealer to the scrap heap will provide a talking
point for a party, a gimmick to amuse and impress friends. Spending of this sort, which is made without regard for the investment
aspect of art, is no more than the froth on the current boom and
might be expected to stop at the first signs of serious economic
difficulties. But, looking back over the past few years, we see that
the boom generally is of a much sounder nature. Indeed, it becomes apparent that, up to a point, the art market thrives on stock-
market setbacks.

In his *Art as an Investment* Richard H. Rush quotes an official
of one of the largest galleries in the world as saying that in the
recession of 1957 he was literally deluged with Wall Street brokers
wanting to buy paintings. And in 1962, in the period following
Black Tuesday (May 29), the London art market remained surprisingly buoyant. On June 14 of that year Sotheby's sold the
Alexander Korda collection of Impressionist and Post-Impression-

ist pictures for £464,470 and then threw a lavish party for their clients. At that event I found myself sitting next to a somewhat depressed Mr. Charles Clore, a millionaire collector of some discernment, who a few minutes earlier had been the underbidder (at £26,000) for a £28,000 Soutine. I asked him why he had allowed the picture to get away and he replied, "Who has got that sort of money at a time like this?"

Well, it was obvious that somebody had "that sort of money" and lots more besides, for in the same sale £80,000 had been paid for a van Gogh still life and £72,000 for a Degas nude. The results in general suggested that Mr. Clore's reaction to the bad news was the exception rather than the rule and that it would probably take a month of Black Tuesdays to cause panic in the art market.* This was demonstrated again in 1965 when, with the Labour Government wielding the capital-gains-tax stick, and with rumors of devaluation and forecasts of disaster emanating almost daily from the City, the art market registered no serious adverse effects. On the contrary, every cry of woe from the Stock Exchange was countered by a whoop of joy at some new record price paid in the Bond Street and King Street market places.

The headlines on facing pages of an evening newspaper one day in July 1965 summed up the situation succinctly. "Leading Shares Slip Back Again," said the first; "£88,000 for a Turner— Increase of £78,000 in 20 years," read the second. The profit ratios on Rembrandts and Renoirs looked even better than those on property. As a hedge against the vagaries of the stock market, art seemed unbeatable. Tycoons with pretensions to culture were reminded that in the Great Depression of the twenties and thirties

---

* It is of interest to note here that Renoir's *Jeunes Filles au bord de l'eau*, which fetched £42,000 ($117,600) in the Korda sale, made only $57,500 when resold at the Parke-Bernet Galleries, New York, in December 1965.

important works of art held their values better than almost anything else, and they acted accordingly.

But can we be sure that in another economic depression the
same thing would happen? I think we can. For one reason, at
least, we may even take it that art will weather the next great
depression rather better than it did the last. The reason is that
today there are vastly more people who want to own masterpieces
(whether by Old, Impressionist or modern masters) than there
were thirty-five years ago. These people are spread out over most
countries of the world and would all be affected simultaneously
only by an economic disaster of global proportions.

M. Maurice Rheims, the famous French auctioneer, takes an
even more sanguine point of view. In his book *Art on the Market*
he writes:

A major slump [in the art market] today would have sociological
rather than financial implications, for it would take an extraordinary
caprice of taste before the world-wide passion for works of art became
transmuted into a general indifference . . . Such an eventuality could
only be the outcome of a fundamental change in the human way of
life, perhaps the result of fantastic new discoveries which might make
a work of art superfluous and derisory.

As I have shown in Chapter Fourteen, there are many forces
already at work to bring about the eventuality to which M. Rheims
refers. It is an eventuality which I believe is inevitable but much
too far off to worry the good art-gamesman and send him running
for the first train to New Babylon. Even so it seems to me that
M. Rheims is a little too optimistic and that a word of warning
should be given to the hundreds of thousands of people who are
playing the art game on a lower plane than the "International
League" level.

Obviously the wide international market that is the collector's insurance against a depression in his own country will be interested only in the work of artists of international repute, which generally means the great masters of all periods. But in countries like Britain, France, America, Italy there are enormous sums of money invested by collectors in the work of native artists who are completely unknown outside their own countries. Such collectors will clearly be the most vulnerable in the event of an economic depression of only national proportions. Only a damn-fool art investor will, therefore, allow himself to be influenced by patriotism in making his collection. The wise one will aim always to possess things that have an "international rating." He will aim, too, at owning works of the highest possible quality and, contrary to the advice of Mr. Rush, will prefer to put all his eggs into one first-class basket than to share them among a dozen inferior ones. And he will feel safe only when he has an undisputed masterpiece (or several masterpieces) that makes other men like him all over the world feel sick with envy. Even then he would do well not to forget that "fashion is a sorcerer's charm or talisman changing the masterpieces of today into the laughing stock of tomorrow,"* and that it is conceivable that even the greatest Old Masters may be again, as they have been in the past, subject to the whims of fashion.

---

* Maurice Rheims, *Art on the Market*.

Bibliography

BOOKS

Alloway, Lawrence, *Nine Abstract Artists*. London: Alec Tiranti Ltd., 1954.

Bainbridge, John, *The Super-Americans*. London: Gollancz, 1962.

Barber, Noël, *Conversations with Painters*. London: Collins, 1964.

Behrman, S. N., *Duveen*. London: Hamish Hamilton, 1952; London: Arrow Books Ltd., 1960, paperback.

Bell, Clive, *Art*. London: Chatto and Windus, 1914; New Edition 1949.

Brockwell, Maurice, *The Pseudo-Arnolfini Portrait*. London: Chatto and Windus, 1952.

Carter, A. C. R., *Let Me Tell You*. London: Hutchinson, 1942.

Churchill, Winston, *Painting as a Pastime*. New York: McGraw-Hill, 1950; Cornerstone Library, 1965.

Fischer, Ernst, *The Necessity of Art: A Marxist Approach*. Harmondsworth, Middlesex: Penguin Books, 1963.

Fry, Roger, *Vision and Design*. Harmondsworth, Middlesex: Penguin Books, 1937.

Guggenheim, Peggy, *Confessions of an Art Addict*. London: André Deutsch Ltd., 1960.

Hendy, Philip, *The National Gallery, London*. London: Thames and Hudson, 1960.

217

Holmes, Sir Charles, *Pictures and Picture Collecting*. London: Anthony Treherne and Co., Ltd., 1903.

Johns, Geoffrey, *Any Advance?* London: Hutchinson, 1962.

Meadmore, W. S., *Lucien Pissarro*. London: Constable and Co., 1962.

Reitlinger, Gerald, *The Economics of Taste*. London: Barrie and Rockliff, 1961.

Rheims, Maurice, *Art on the Market*. London: Weidenfeld and Nicolson, 1961.

Rosenberg, Harold, *The Anxious Object*. London: Thames and Hudson, 1965.

Rush, Richard H., *Art as an Investment*. Englewood Cliffs, New Jersey: Prentice Hall, Inc., 1961.

Schüller, Sepp, *Forgers, Dealers, Experts*. London: Arthur Barker, 1960.

Shahn, Ben, *The Shape of Content*. Cambridge, Mass.: Harvard University Press; New York: Vintage Books, 1960.

Thoene, Peter, *Modern German Art*. Harmondsworth, Middlesex: Penguin Books, 1938.

Wynne-Morgan, John, *Oil Paintings as a Pastime*. London: Souvenir Press Ltd., 1959.

PERIODICALS

Ark. (The magazine of students of The Royal College of Art, London), No. 35, 1964.

Art News. New York, issue of February 1964.

Arts & Architecture. Los Angeles, issue of October 1961.

Art Voices. New York, issue of November 1962.

ICA Bulletin. Publication of the Institute of Contemporary Arts, London.

The Studio. London, issues of July 1929 and June 1962.

Index

Abrams, Harry, 64
Abstractionists, 54, 55
Agnew, Geoffrey, 36, 141, 147
Agnew, Hugh, 116
Agnew & Sons, Thomas, 33, 36, 60, 143, 144, 148, 149, 152, 161, 185
Alloway, Lawrence, 169
Alma-Tadema, Sir Lawrence, 52, 56
Alte Pinakothek, 91
Alwyn, William, 47–49
"American Death Show," exhibition, 202
Andrea del Sarto, 81
Angerstein, John Julius, 21–22
Annigoni, Pietro, 17, 31, 59
Antico, 123
Ark, 199
Arp, Jean, 55
Art International, 201
Art Nouveau, 49
Art Voices, 164
Ashton, Dore, 6, 166, 172
Atkinson, Terry, 199

Bache, Jules, 23, 24
Bacon, Francis, 55, 65, 158, 188

Bainbridge, John, 26
Balla, Giacomo, 55
Balthus, 55
Barber, Noël, 15
Baring, Major Edward, 36
Bartolommeo, Fra, 143
Baudelaire, Charles, 6, 175
Baur, John I. H., 62
Baziotes, William, 69
Beckmann, Max, 55
Behrman, S. N., 13
Bell, Clive, 188, 192, 195, 196
Bell, Vanessa, 58
Bellini, Giovanni, 90
Bellotto, Bernardo, 76, 77
Benjamin-Constant, J., 59
Berchem, Nicolas, 54
Berenson, Bernard, 89, 90
Berger, John, 82
Birch, S. J. Lamorna, 171
Birmingham City Art Gallery, 124
Blake, William, 41, 51, 55
Blakelock, Ralph A., 56
Blanche, Jacques Emile, 57
Bloch, Martin, 57
Blok, C., 6, 18
Boccioni, Umberto, 55
Boggs, Frank, 57
Bomberg, David, 57

Bonham's (W. & F. C. Bonham & Sons Ltd.) 135
Bonheur, Rosa, 59
Bonnard, Pierre, 39, 41
Boudin, Eugène, 39
Bouguereau, W. A., 59
Bouts, Dirck, 121
Bowstead, John, 199
Brabazon, Hercules Brabazoz, 58
Brancusi, Constantin, 54, 168
Braque, Georges, 39, 41, 42, 54, 179, 207
Bratby, John, 58
Brausen, Erica, 159
Brecht, Bertolt, 199
Breton, Jules, 59
British Antique Dealers Association, 115, 116
British Broadcasting Corporation, 174
British Council, 170
British Insurance Association, 183
British Museum, 81, 93
Brockwell, Maurice, 184
Brooking, Charles, 44
Brouwn, Stanley, 210
Brown, Ford Madox, 47, 48, 56, 120

Brown, Frederick, 57
Buffet, Bernard, 59
Bunton, Kempton, 179, 184
Burne-Jones, Sir Edward, 47, 48, 56
Bury, Pol, 206

Calder, Alexander, 207
Cameron, Sir David Young, 57
Canaletto (Antonio Canal), 76, 77
Carter, A. C. R., 185
Cary, Joyce, 198
Cézanne, Paul, 32, 41, 42, 128, 172, 173, 180
Chagall, Marc, 55, 64, 179
Chamberlain, John, 204
Chance, I. O. ("Peter"), 141, 142
Chandron, André, 178
Chapman, Joe, 177
Chardin, Jean Baptiste Siméon, 120
Charles I, King of England, 19, 124
Charles II, King of England, 20, 21
Christie's, 12, 35, 36, 38, 44, 48, 50, 60, 65, 75, 76, 86, 90, 108, 110, 112, 113, 114, 117, 124, 127, 128, 129, 135, 140-2, 148, 149, 152, 154, 155, 156, 185
Churchill, Sir Winston, 192, 195
Clark, Sir Kenneth, 80, 119
Claude (Gellée or Lorrain), 120, 124, 154
Clausen, Sir George, 57
Cleveland Museum of Art, 90, 92
Clore, Charles, 213
Clough, Prunella, 58
Collier, John, 57
Colnaghi, P. & D., 140, 144
Colombe d'Or, 179, 180, 192
Colquhoun, Robert, 58

Connard, Sir Philip, 58
Constable, John, 77, 78, 98, 120
Cook, Lady, 143
Cook, Sir Francis, 143
Cook Collection, 140
Cooper, Thomas Sidney, 57
Corot, Jean Baptiste Camille, 55, 73, 74, 78, 80, 106, 107
Correggio, Antonio, 124
Cotman, John Sell, 107
Coward, Noël, 60
Cowdray, Lord, 60
Cox, David, 77
Cozens, Alexander, 123
Cromwell, Oliver, 20
Cross, Henri Edmond, 57
Cubism, 207
Cundall, Charles, 120

Dadaists, 203
Dadd, Richard, 41, 51, 55, 104
Daily Express, 181, 182
Daily Mail, 120
Daily Telegraph, 6, 38, 199
Dali, Salvador, 87
Daubigny, Charles François, 56
Daumier, Honoré, 55, 95, 96
Davidson, Marshall B., 12
Davies, Arthur B., 56
Davis, Stuart, 69
Day, James Wentworth, 120
De Blaas, Eugène, 59
Degas, Hilaire Germain Edgar, 194, 213
De Glehn, W. G., 57
De Kooning, Willem, 63, 64, 65, 69
Delacroix, Eugène, 42, 55, 73
De Largillière, Nicolas, 35, 36
Delug, A., 59
Derain, André, 55

De Segonzac, André Dunoyer, 180, 181
De Staël, Nicolas, 55
De Wint, Peter, 77, 78, 107
Diaz de la Peña, Narcisse Virgil, 56
Diderot, Denis, 175
Dine, Jim, 70, 204
Dobell, William, 57
Dobson, Frank, 57, 58
Dove, Arthur, 69
Drysdale, Russell, 57
Duchamp, Marcel, 18
Dufy, Raoul, 55
Dunlop, R. O., 58
Dürer, Albrecht, 122
Duveen, Lord (Joseph), 6, 22-24, 30, 33, 37, 89, 91, 144, 149, 155, 163

École de Paris, 51, 54, 55, 150
Egg, Augustus Leopold, 120
Epstein, Jacob, 57, 104, 176
Erickson, Alfred W., 33
Ernst, Max, 55, 205
Etty, William, 56
Evening News (London), 177, 179
Evening Standard (London), 121

Fildes, Sir Luke, 59
Fine Artz Associates, 199, 206, 208
Firle, Walther, 59
Fischer, Ernst, 197, 209
Fischer, Harry, 151
Fisher, Mark, 57
Flandrin, P. H., 59
"Flint Jack," 80
Flint, Sir William Russell, 50, 60
Fontana, Lucio, 204
Forain, Jean-Louis, 56
Foster, Myles Birket, 107
Francia, Francesco, 90
Francis, Sam, 65, 69
Freud, Clement, 161-2
Frick, Henry Clay, 23, 24

Frith, William Powell, 49, 56
Fry, Roger, 170
Furse, Charles, 57
Fuseli, Henry, 56
Futurists, 55, 207

Gainsborough, Thomas, 23, 31, 33, 119, 120, 185
Gallery One, London, 201
Gaudier-Brzeska, Henri, 57, 122
Gauguin, Paul, 32, 35, 41, 42
Geest, Willem, 59
Gellée, *see* Claude
Gemeente Museum, The Hague, 18
German Expressionists, 51, 55
Gertrude Stein Gallery, 202
Getty, Paul, 91, 92, 93, 101
Giacometti, Alberto, 55
Gill, Eric, 58
Gimpel, Charles, 159
Gimpel Fils, 159
Gimpel, Peter, 159
Giorgione, 20, 89, 90
Girtin, Thomas, 120
Glarner, Fritz, 69
Glover, John, 56
Goenuette, Norbert, 56
Goering, Hermann, 88
Goldschmidt sale, 38, 41, 128, 129
Goodall, Frederick, 59
Goodwin, Albert, 58
Gorky, Arshile, 69
Gosse, Sylvia, 58
Gottlieb, Adolph, 65, 69
Goya, Francisco, 41, 119, 179, 180, 181, 182, 184, 185
Grant, Duncan, 57
Greuze, Jean Baptiste, 120
Grimshaw, Atkinson, 57
Gromaire, Marcel, 57
Grosvenor Gallery, London, 168
"Group N" of Padua, 207
"Group T" of Milan, 207

Guggenheim, Peggy, 6, 9, 204, 205
Guillaumin, Armand, 56, 73
Gunn, Sir James, 122
Guston, Philip, 65, 69
Guthrie, Sir James, 59

Hall, Dr. Edward, 94
Hallsborough Gallery, London, 154, 155
Hals, Frans, 41
Hanover Gallery, London, 159
"Happenings Movement," 13, 210
Harpignies, Henri, 56
Haupt Collection, Ira, 65
Healey, John, 207
Hébert, A. E., 59
Hendy, Sir Philip, 22, 77, 90
Henry, Prince of Wales, 19
Henry VIII, King of England, 19
Hepworth, Barbara, 57, 188
Hilton, Roger, 169, 204
Hirshhorn, Joe, 164
Hitler, Adolf, 31
Hockney, David, 189
Hoenich, P. K., 146, 207
Hofmann, Hans, 69
Hogarth, William, 120, 140
Holbein, Hans (the Younger), 20
Holl, Frank, 59
Holmes, Sir Charles, 117
"Homo ludens," 208, 210
Horner, E. A., 59
Horton, W. S., 56
Hughes, Arthur, 56
Hunt, William Holman, 31, 48, 56
Huntington, Henry E., 23, 24, 33

Ibbetson, Julius Caesar, 56, 156
ICA Bulletin, 209

Illustrated Weekly of India, The, 164
Impressionists and Impressionism, 41, 42, 49, 51, 194
Intimists, 54
Isabey, Eugène, 57
Israels, Josef, 56

Jandolo, Augusto, 79, 107
Jawlensky, Alexej von, 55
"Jean Gros-Tête," 182
Jeannerat, Pierre, 117, 119, 122
Jeffs, Roger, 199
Jennings, Bernard, 199
John, Augustus, 60, 84, 95, 106
John, D'Oyly, 50
John, Gwen, 57
Johns, Geoffrey, 111
Johns, Jasper, 70
Jones, David, 57

Kaiser Friedrich Museum, Berlin, 81
Kandinsky, Wassily, 31, 54
Kaprow, Allan, 203
Kasmin Gallery, London, 66
Kauffmann, Angelica, 56
Kirchner, Ernst Ludwig, 55
Kisling, Moïse, 57
Klee, Paul, 31, 55
Klein, Yves, 42, 202
Kline, Franz, 63, 69
Knoedler Bros., 23, 144
Koetser, Leonard, 90
Kokoschka, Oskar, 31, 55, 188
Korda Collection sale, 212–213
Kraushar, Leon, 64
Kress, Samuel, 24
Krieghoff, Cornelius, 123
Kunsthalle, Bremen, 90
Kunsthalle, Hamburg, 154
Kupka, Frantisek (Frank), 55

Lagar, Celso, 57
Lamb, Henry, 58
Landseer, Sir Edwin, 25, 49, 56
Lanyon, Peter, 57
Latham, John, 204
La Thangue, H. H., 59
Latour, Madame Claude, 83
Laver, James, 48, 49, 52, 58
Lavery, Sir John, 57
Lawrence, D. H., 57, 164
Lawrence, Sir Thomas, 76
Lear, Edward, 156
Lebourg, Albert, 57
Lefèvre Gallery, London, 44
Léger, Fernand, 87, 179
Legros, Alphonse, 58
Leighton, Lord, 52, 56
Leonardo da Vinci, 16, 20, 34, 41, 42, 43, 81, 82, 172; *Mona Lisa*, 177–9, 181, 201
Leopold William of Austria, Archduke, 20
Lépine, Stanislas, 56, 120
Leslie, C. R., 56
Lessore, Thérèse, 58
Lévis, Maurice, 57
Life International, 63
Lloyd, Frank, 151
Loiseau, Gustave, 57
Long, Edwin, 59
Lorrain, *see* Claude
Louis, Morris, 69
Louvre, The, 177, 178, 180
Lucas, Albert Dürer, 82
Luce, Maximilien, 57, 71, 72, 73, 74
Lowry, Laurence Stephen, 41, 44, 57, 84
"Lumino-dynamic constructions," 206
"Luminous pictures," 207

Maeght, Aimé, 179, 180
Maillol, Aristide, 95
Maitland, Paul, 58
Mané-Katz, 57

Manet, Edouard, 41, 98, 128, 173
Manzoni, Piero, 18
Marc, Franz, 165, 199
Marchand, Jean, 57
Marin, John, 69
Maris Brothers, 59
Marlborough Fine Art Ltd., 47, 66, 141, 151, 158, 159, 160, 162, 188, 190
Marlborough-Gerson Gallery, 66
Marquet, Albert, 55
Marshall, Ben, 103–4
Martens, Willy, 59
Martin, Sir Alec, 38
Martin, Fritz, 73
Martin, John ("Mad"), 51, 56
Masaccio, 91
Mathieu, Georges, 59
Matisse, Henri, 41, 42, 54, 74, 95, 96
Maugham, Somerset, 186
Mazarin, Cardinal, 20
Maze, Paul, 58
McEvoy, Ambrose, 57, 58
Meadmore, W. S., 97–8
Mellon, Andrew, 23, 24, 33, 89, 90
Meninsky, Bernard, 58
Mesdag, H. W., 59
Metropolitan Museum, New York, 118
Michelangelo, 41, 42, 43
Millais, Sir John Everett, 48, 56
Millares, Manolo, 204
Millet, Jean François, 55
"Milliprobe," 94
Ministry of Fine Arts, France, 181
Miró, Joan, 54, 205
Modigliani, Amedeo, 41, 54, 64
Mondrian, Piet, 54, 209
Monet, Claude, 42, 64, 171
Monticelli, Adolphe, 56
Moore, Albert, 25, 55, 56

Moore, Henry, 44, 55, 57, 65, 122, 124, 188
Morgan, Fred, 59
Morland, George, 56, 76
Mote, G. W., 56
Motherwell, Robert, 69
Mullaly, Terence, 6, 38
Müller, W. J., 59
Mundy, Henry, 204
Munnings, Sir Alfred, 50, 60, 106, 107

Nan Kivell, Rex de C., 47
Nash, Paul, 104
Nasmyth, Alexander, 56
Nasmyth, Patrick, 56, 77, 78
National Art Collections Fund, 34
National Gallery, London, 22, 33, 34, 41, 77, 90, 91, 94, 100, 119, 122, 132, 179, 181, 187
National Gallery, Washington, 89
National Museum of Wales, 180
Neo-Dadaists, 201, 203
Nepote, Jean, 181
Nevinson, C. R. W., 57
"New Babylon," 171, 208, 209, 214
Newman, Barnett, 63, 64, 69
New Realists, 52, 201, 203
New Yorker, The, 89
"New York School," 17, 190
Niarchos, Stavros, 34
Nicholson, Ben, 50, 55, 158, 188, 189
Nicholson, Sir William, 58
Nicholson, Winifred, 58
Nieuwenhuys, Constant, 208, 210
Nolan, Sidney, 57
Noland, Kenneth, 69
Nolde, Emil, 31, 55
Nonnenbruch, Max, 59
Northwick Collection, 121
"No Show," exhibition, 202

Observer, The, 177
O'Hana, Jacques, 87, 183
O'Hana Gallery, London, 87, 162, 182, 185
Oldenburg, Claes, 63, 64, 70, 204
Oliver, Peter, 124
"Op" art, 52, 68
Opie, John, 120
Orpen, Sir William, 58

Palma Vecchio, 90
Palmer, Samuel, 41, 51, 55, 123
Parke-Bernet Galleries, 65, 135, 213
Parsons, Alfred, 58
Partridge & Sons, Frank, 36
Pascin (Julius Pincas), 55
Pasmore, Victor, 31
Pavillon de Vendôme, Aix, 180
Pearson, John, 148
Peppercorn, Adrian, 58
Permeke, Constant, 57
Perugia, Vicenzo, 177, 178
"Peter Simple," 200–1
Pether, Sebastian, 56
Pétridès, Paul, 83
Philip IV, King of Spain, 20
Phillips, Son & Neale, 135
Picasso, Pablo, 26, 39, 41, 42, 51, 53, 54, 64, 84, 87, 99, 166, 171, 172, 173, 175, 179, 186, 197, 205, 207
Piene, Otto, 204
Pissarro, Camille, 25, 97, 171
Pissarro, Lucien, 97–8
Pochkanawala, Pilloo, 164
Poliakoff, Serge, 59
Pollock, Jackson, 42, 46, 65, 69, 204
"Pop" art, 52, 63, 64, 66, 68, 203
Pope-Hennessy, John, 118
Porkay, Martin, 90
Portal Gallery, London, 51

Portobello Road, 125
Post-Impressionists, 40, 41, 42, 49, 51
Poynter, Sir Edward, 59
Pre-Raphaelites, 41, 47, 48, 50, 192
Prout, Margaret Fisher, 120
"Pubists," 52
Puvis de Chavannes, Pierre, 56

Queen, The, 161

Raffaëlli, Jean-François, 56
"Random" art, 207
Raphael, 20, 31, 33, 41, 42, 43, 81, 93
Rauschenberg, Robert, 64, 197, 204
Read, Sir Herbert, 173, 196
Redfern Gallery, London, 47
Reinhardt, Ad, 17, 188
Reitlinger, Gerald, 6, 13, 19
Rembrandt, 12, 19, 33, 41, 43, 81, 90, 91, 119, 124, 213; portrait of Titus, 140–3
Renoir, Pierre Auguste, 31, 41, 42, 128, 161, 162, 173, 213
Reynolds, Alan, 31
Reynolds, Sir Joshua, 120
Rheims, Maurice, 40, 214, 215
Richards, Ceri, 50, 158
Richardson, Sir Albert, 119
Richelieu, Cardinal, 20
Ricketts, Charles, 58
Ridley, Nicholas, 116
Riley, Bridget, 189
Riopelle, Jean-Paul, 59
Rivers, Larry, 66
Rivière, Briton, 59
Roberts, David, 56
Roberts, William, 58
Rodin, Auguste, 55
Rosenberg, Harold, 67, 68

Rosenquist, James, 63
Rossetti, Dante Gabriel, 55
Rosso, Medardo, 55
Rothko, Mark, 63, 69
Rouault, Georges, 55
Rousseau, Théodore, 56
Rouve, Pierre, 168
Rowlandson, Thomas, 56
Royal Academy of Arts, 16, 34, 49, 119, 171
Royal College of Art, 189
Rush, Richard H., 6, 30–32, 46, 212, 215
Rushbury, Sir Henry, 120
Ruskin, John, 81, 163
Ryder, Albert Pinkham, 56

Sandby, Paul, 106, 107
Sassoon, Siegfried, 104
Savery, Roelandt, 54
Schecroun, Jean-Pierre, 82, 87
Schiller, Friedrich, 175
Schmidt-Rottluff, Karl, 55
Schöffer, Nicholas, 207
Schüller, Sepp, 88
Schwitters, Kurt, 197, 204
Scull, Robert C., 63, 64, 65, 66
Shahn, Ben, 6, 70, 164, 191–2, 197
Shannon, Charles, 58
Shayer, William, 56
Sickert, Walter Richard, 57, 58, 98, 104
Simon, Norton, 12, 140–2
Sims, Charles, 58
Sironi, Mario, 57, 168
Sisley, Alfred, 171
Smith, David, 69
Smith, Jack, 14–15, 58
Smith, Sir Matthew, 104
Snyders, Frans, 92
Solomon, Solomon J., 59
Somerset, The Hon. David, 141–2
Sotheby & Co., 6, 10, 35, 36, 37, 38, 43, 44, 47, 48, 60, 65, 75, 76, 77, 93, 97, 104, 108, 110,

112, 113, 114, 122, 124,
125, 126, 127, 128, 129,
131, 135, 142, 148, 149,
152, 155, 156
Soulages, Pierre, 59
Soutine, Chaïm, 41, 47,
54, 213
Souza, Francis Newton,
58, 197
Spear, Ruskin, 58
Spencer, Stanley, 31, 41,
104
Spencer-Churchill, Capt.
E. G., 115, 121, 122
Spink & Son, Ltd., 161, 162
Stanfield, W. Clarkson, 58
Stark, James, 56
Steer, Philip Wilson, 31,
57, 106
Stella, Joseph, 69
Still, Clyfford, 64, 65, 69
Stott, Edward, 59
Studio, The, 164
Stück, Franz, 59
Sunday Express, 91
Sunday Telegraph, 182
Sunday Times, 113, 114,
115
Surrealists, 54, 203
Sutherland, Graham, 50,
57, 158, 188, 189
Sutton, Philip, 58
Swebach, called Fontaine,
Jacques-François-Jose,
120
Swynnerton, Annie Louisa,
59

Takis, 206
Tate Gallery, 13, 47, 70,
104, 167, 168
Teniers, David (the Elder),
76
Teniers, David (the Youn-
ger), 54, 76, 109, 120
Tertis, Lionel, 124

Thompson, Peter, 80–1
Thyssen Collection, 100
Time, 62
Tinguely, Jean, 204
Tissot, James J., 56
Titian, 20, 89, 90, 121
Tobey, Mark, 64, 65, 69
Tolstoy, Count Leo, 71
Tonks, Henry, 58
Tooth, Dudley, 140, 142
Tooth's Gallery, London,
51, 60, 162
Toulouse-Lautrec, Henri
de, 42
Towne, Francis, 107
Tretchikoff, 50
Trigoulet, Eugène, 59
Troyon, Constantin, 56
Trübner, W., 59
Turner, Joseph Mallord
William, 42, 76, 77, 81,
102, 213
Turner, William (Turner
of Oxford), 76
Tuscany, Grand Duke of,
20

Utrillo, Maurice, 41, 83,
84

Van der Ast, Balthasar,
130, 132, 136
Van Dongen, Kees, 55
Van Dyck, Sir Anthony, 92
Van Eyck, Hubert, 184
Van Eyck, Jan, 91, 184
Van Eyck "brothers," 184
Van Gogh, Vincent, 32, 73,
128, 213
Van Goyen, Jan, 84, 86,
87, 120
Van Huysum, Jan, 130–3,
138
Van Meegeren, Han, 79,
80, 82, 87, 88, 94

Van Ostade, Adriaen, 54,
76
Van Verendael, Nicolas,
122
Vaughan, Keith, 58
Vauthier, Ben, 201–2
Venice Biennale, 26
Vermeer, Jan, 88
Vernet, Joseph, 120
Victoria and Albert Mu-
seum, 20, 48, 118, 122
Vlaminck, Maurice, 41, 55
Volz, Wilhelm, 59
Von Bode, Wilhelm, 21,
81, 82
Von Uhde, Fritz, 59
Vuillard, Edouard, 39, 41,
54

Walker, Dame Ethel, 51,
58
Walker, Frederick, 59
Wallis, Alfred, 41
Wall Street Journal, 30–1,
33
Ward, James, 55
Warhol, Andy, 64, 69, 70
Watts, F. W., 56
Watts, George Frederick,
59
Wellington, Duke of, 179
Wesselman, Tom, 64
West, Benjamin, 120
Wilde, Oscar, 40
Wildenstein, 144, 161
Williams, William (Wil-
liams of Norwich), 125
Wilson, Peter, 6, 19, 34,
36, 37, 127, 128, 135
Wilson, Richard, 54, 120
Wilson, "Scottie," 164
Worth, Adam, 185
Wouwerman, Philips, 54,
120
Wynne-Morgan, John, 194
Wyeth, Andrew, 70